ON AND OFF THE RECORD: COLOSI ON NEGOTIATION

By Thomas R. Colosi

Second Edition

American Arbitration Association
Dispute Resolution Services Worldwide

Second Edition; Revised August 2001

For information, contact the
    American Arbitration Association
    Publications Dept.
    335 Madison Avenue
    New York, N.Y. 10017
    Phone: (212) 716-3968

Legal forms pictured on cover by Julius Blumberg, Inc., New York, NY

Library of Congress Catalog Card Number: 91-76091

ISBN 0-8403-8585-4

Printed in the United States of America
10 9 8 7 6 5

DEDICATION

To Robert Coulson, former AAA president, who gave me constant encouragement and the "elbow room" to allow for the development of the methodologies and principles set forth in this book.

AUTHOR'S ACKNOWLEDGMENT

To Professor Jack Wood of the International Institute for Management Development (IIMB) in Switzerland for patiently sitting through many of my lectures in order to capture the common threads that weave their way through this book and for his sage advice.

To Ann Thomas, mediator and former editor of the *Society of Professionals in Dispute Resolution (SPIDR) Newsletter*, for her exceptional effort helping to organize the material for this book and in the initial editing of it.

To Dr. Arthur E. Berkeley, arbitrator and faculty member of Memphis State University, for his contributions in editing and helping to integrate the material during a later stage of development.

Thanks to Jack A. Smith, former editorial director, and Dorissa Bolinski, former copy editor, of the AAA Publications Department, and to Anne Burson, my assistant, for their editorial skill and patience. Thanks to Ted Pons, vice president of the AAA Publications Department, for his cooperation and encouragement.

PARADIGM SHIFT

In an article in the *Cleveland Plain Dealer* on Jan. 10, 1993, titled "Old Ideas are Powerful Restraints," David Osborne* discussed the meaning of a paradigm shift. He wrote:

> The word paradigm was popularized by Thomas Kuhn in his 1962 book, *The Structure of Scientific Revolutions*. A paradigm, as Kuhn defined it, is a set of assumptions about reality—an accepted mode or pattern—that explains the world better than any other set of assumptions.
>
> In science, Kuhn's subject, each paradigm has its own set of rules and illuminates its own set of facts. As long as it explains most observed phenomena and solves the problems most people want solved, it remains dominant. But as new phenomena begin to contradict it, the paradigm succumbs to increasing doubt. As these "anomalies" multiply, it is thrown into crisis. Finally someone articulates a new paradigm, and a broad shift takes place.
>
> Kuhn argued that human beings deal with social reality in much the same way—"that something like a paradigm is prerequisite to perception itself. What a man sees depends both upon what he looks at and also upon what his previous visual-conceptual experience has taught him to see."

Osborne's main point was to explain why even though "It's easy to dream up new approaches to problems…The hard part is selling them to those who still see the world through old lenses. Why? Because the transformation from bureaucratic to entrepreneurial government (the subject of Osborne's article) is not just a change—it is a shift in world view. It is a world paradigm shift."

On and Off the Record is intended to change readers' minds about the negotiation process. It is common for negotiators to approach the process with an inappropriate number of views, which forms an incomplete paradigm. This negatively affects the behavior of parties to a negotiation and creates unnecessary problems for the negotiator. Our society relies on negotiating skills for conducting all manners of business and personal transactions, yet, it is only just beginning to learn and to teach the negotiation process.

The greatest misunderstanding about the negotiation process is that it is adversarial in nature. In actuality, it is not designed for those with a trial and debate mentality. It is a problem-solving process in which each party may look across the table and regard its counterparts as advocates. Each party attempts to "sell" a mutually agreed upon solution to its respective clients. Seeing the "other side" as a potential advocate and not as an opponent is the key to *making* this dramatic paradigm shift.

* David Osborne is a contributing editor of *Governing Magazine* and co-author, with Ted Gaebler, of the 1992 book, *Reinventing Government: How the Entrepreneurial Spirit is Transforming the Public Sector*.

NEGOTIATION PRAYER

Please give me patience…
and I want it right now!
—Anonymous

ABOUT THE TITLE

The author admits that the title of "On and Off the Record" is intended to initially attract potential buyers who are beginning to perceive serious negotiations as those discussions that transpire not only across the negotiation table, but also off the record. In reality, the more serious discussions usually take place off the record away from the negotiating table. They may occur over the telephone, in a corridor, in a cloak room, in a parking lot, in a restaurant, etc. These types of negotiations may be direct negotiations or one-on-one, those involving a mediator between the chief spokesperson from each side or those occuring two-on-two rather than team-on-team.

Serious negotiations also occur between representatives who are sent "to the table" and ratifiers who send their representatives "to the table." The pros and cons of this more realistic and less simplistic version of the negotiating process are discussed in this book. Also noted are the ways successful negotiators move from position-based and interest-based bargaining, which usually occur at the table, to expectation-based bargaining, which generally takes place away from the table when negotiators negotiate with their counterparts off the record. Off-the-record negotiation is discussed throughout the book and also in Appendix D, "The Iceberg Principle: Secrecy in Negotiation."

Finally, the concept of negotiating both on and off the record can be applied to negotiations that occur within and between levels of an organization, a subject addressed in this book as well.

Contents

Foreword

This book describes how you can conduct an effective negotiation and how you and the other party or parties can get what you want (or rather, what you think you want), in the process. How? By describing the process, structure and management of negotiation.

Negotiation as a topic of study has obviously come of age. Bookstore shelves are beginning to groan with the weight of negotiation books. Every month, more magazine articles on negotiation appear. But most of these books and articles only discuss techniques for influencing others.

They contain principles, precepts, warnings, rules and lists of do's and don'ts. A few coach you on how to manage or control your information and timing, such as when to make an offer. Some even tell you how to misrepresent your true interests. Others tell you how to make the quick killing—how to posture, "wheedle," intimidate and bluff. Books with a longer view tell you how to maintain a relationship with the other party while you attend to your interests, assuming you have thought about and understand your interests and their interests.

This book attempts to go beyond that. It explains how to identify, understand and manage the many relationships and aspects that come into play all around you as part of the negotiation process. It identifies what you need to know to conduct a negotiation successfully, as a music director conducts a symphony—orchestrating the various instruments and voices to create a coherent harmony.

Think of this book as a tool, and as with any tool, it can be used to build and maintain relationships and transactions, but many of the concepts can be misused by those who are ill-intended. It is the author's wish that the concepts in this book are used with the very best intentions.

To The Reader

This book is written from the point of view of one who has lived and worked professionally as a negotiator and a mediator in our Western society. Since basic human behavior is similar from culture to culture, the majority of the principles I espouse will be easily understood from Western and Eastern Europe to the Middle East. Some practices mentioned might seem unacceptable to certain cultures due to indigenous behavior—I will leave the chore of utilizing said principles and practices to those authors most familiar with the negotiating processes as practiced in those societies.

In this book, I make a major point of bifurcating the negotiation process into the actual negotiation stage and the ratification stage. Thus, when I refer to the "ratifier," I will use many different labels, such as the "closer," the "client," the one who "blesses" the deal, the "boss," "headquarters," and, of course, the ratifier, depending on the context. To explain why I feel this bifurcation is critical, let me paraphrase Abraham Lincoln's well-known statement: "Any person who represents themselves has a fool for a client." He said it all.

I struggled long and hard not to title this book, "The Negotiation Process: Table Manners." In my 35 years at the negotiating table, I have learned that those who attempt to intimidate, yell, debate, insult or generally engage in negative behavior designed to destabilize those across the table usually work against their basic interests if their interest is to get a deal and if they eventually want the deal implemented. I have found that there is a direct relationship between their demonstrated negative behavior and the amount of time it takes to achieve an acceptable deal, the quality of the deal, and the extent to which the deal will be implemented. To quote another U.S. president in endorsing this principle, Teddy Roosevelt once uttered the famous words: "Speak softly and carry a big stick." This is another important concept that is crucial to effective negotiating. Negative, discourteous behavior usually reveals insecurity and weakness, and those sitting across the table know that.

One last point: in a negotiation, perception is the reality. Many of the negotiator's decisions are based on how he or she feels and to what degree one person can trust another's statements regarding fact, behavior, promises and commitments. Having said that, I believe this book will aid readers in being perceived the way they wish to be perceived, and thus will help them achieve their wants, needs, interests, and expectations.

What You Need to Know to Become an Effective Advocate

Virtually all recent books on the negotiation process have stressed skills, techniques, and ways to prevail over the other side. While such information is valuable, too often the reader is deprived of any underlying theory or rationale beyond simply triumphing over the other side or avoiding the destructive chaos of disagreement through thoughtful damage control.

This book is far different. It provides practical "how to do it" information, but also addresses the more important question of "Why do you do it?" by walking the reader through the maze of the complicated process of negotiation.

This is a book for advocates. It is for advocates whether they are involved in evidentiary processes such as arbitrations, administrative hearings or court trials, or in negotiations such as creating commercial transactions through careful planning, settling disputes and grievances, or finding ways to avoid or solve problems.

When this book was first published in 1993, advocacy training in our competitive society usually focused on how to win in a win/lose forum; essentially, this was the law school approach. In the subsequent eight years, the teaching and learning of the negotiation process and the helper process of mediation has virtually exploded in our schools of law, business, and government. However, I believe we still have a long way to go. While training is abundant on how to research and prepare a case to succeed at trial or arbitration where winning is based on the decision of a third party, there is still very little training on how to succeed in negotiations when winning must be redefined many times to suit the situation.

On the other hand, successful negotiation is not necessarily defined by a win/win outcome. A win/win approach to negotiation is useful only if the parties or disputants take the time to mutually define "winning." The process of negotiation is generally far too complex to squeeze into the two-word phrase win/win. A litigation mind-set *can be* useful in preparing one's case, and that means becoming thoroughly grounded in the law, evidence and proof, issues, defenses and positions of the opposition as well as the expectations of one's own client. In litigation, however, one is constrained by theories that can be supported only by facts which are supported by proof, evidence or testimony. Both must be acceptable under the rules of evidence which would be offered as proof of facts advanced as support for the theory of the case. A neutral trier of fact must be convinced of the viability of the advocate's theory because of the quality of the evidence and the doubt created as to the opposite position. However, if a negotiated outcome is a viable option, the litigation mind-set is much too limited, since the "trier of fact" is not neutral and the "triers of fact" are sitting across the table from one another.

In a negotiation, an advocate must not only prepare both cases, but must achieve something more complicated than convincing or creating doubts in the mind of a neutral third party—an advocate must create doubt in the mind of the opposing advocate, whose position will usually be at strict variance. Further, although facts are used to convince, a fact that is proven through tangible evidence is quite rare in a negotiation. Most information shared in a negotiation is not fact-based but assumption-based, with only the absence of challenge needed to establish an assumption as a fact. Now, it certainly should be easier to create doubt in an assumption than in a fact, since every assumption, by its nature, contains its own seed of doubt. After all, it's only an assumption! But how can one tell the difference between a statement based on assumption rather than fact? On the face of it, you usually cannot, and that is one of the key issues addressed in practical ways in this book.

Negotiation is hard work, but the outcome—a positive relationship with a counterpart who is dedicated to keeping his or her word with you in order for both of your interests to be served—is well worth the time and energy. Often, negotiators spend hours upon hours together. What should the parties be doing to secure this outcome during these endless contact hours?

Building Trust and Relationships

Above all, the negotiators, in every act, word, and deed, must create, build, and maintain trust with the ultimate goal of building a positive relationship. This approach is not advanced for "warm and fuzzy" reasons but is critical for "hardheaded" business reasons alone. The basic job of a negotiator is to persuade, convince, and create doubt and uncertainties in the minds of those who are in disagreement with the negotiator. One cannot effectively create doubts without first creating trust. Those who do not trust the negotiator will not allow the negotiator to create doubts. Therefore, I encourage the reader to become predictable in word, act, and deed, and above all, avoid surprises.

Discovering

Each party should be discovering information the party does not already know. Each party knows what it knows; the purpose of the contact hours with the other party is to find out what that party knows. While a negative relationship will yield little information, a positive relationship will create a freer flow of information through enhanced communication. In a process where information and knowledge are power, a positive relationship is critical.

Educating

Since contact hours should be used to share well-researched information that is designed to make the other party doubt its own information and see things differently if it is in disagreement, it is critical that the other party listen to the new information. Effective listening does not occur within a negative environment. A positive relationship enhances the opportunity for the new information to have maximum impact.

Mutually Defining Facts

During the negotiation, the parties will need to mutually decide what the facts are. What is a fact in a negotiation? In the absence of a third party decider-of-fact, it is really the negotiators themselves who determine the facts of the matter from which decisions are made. Thus, the job of the negotiators is to, as they build a positive relationship, create an environment in which information advanced by one party will be accepted and believed as fact by the other party.

Creating Doubts and Uncertainties

It is important that the effective negotiator create doubts and uncertainties in the parties' minds as to the viability of their positions when appropriate. In a negative relationship, a closed-minded party will not allow doubts to be created. In fact, this party will not become vulnerable enough to allow even modest uncertainties to creep into its mind-set. A change of behavior in the negotiation process is usually preceded by a change in mind-set, and a change in mind-set is preceded by the creation of doubts in that mind-set, which requires a positive, open environment.

Creating Advocacy

In a negotiation, it is rare that the ratifiers engage directly in negotiations during the contact hours. The ratifiers have negotiators (staff or outside consultants) who report to top management (or the constituency/ client(s)) and recommend settlement (or not) under certain conditions. Each negotiating team should attempt to gain advocacy for its position and to take care of its interest in the negotiations with the other negotiating team. It is easier to enlist the other team as your advocate if a positive relationship has been established. Playing the long-term game is important if future implementations are important. As John Galsworthy once said, "If you do not think about the future, you cannot have one."

Behaving Predictably

As an advocate of a more positive approach to resolving disputes, I have been asked many times whether negative behavior—shouts, yelling, insults, intimidations, threats, etc.—are in any way useful in a negotiation relationship. My answer is that if you engage in those kinds of negative behaviors *and you can predict with deadly accuracy* the reaction of the other side to your behavior (and the other side's predicted behavior serves your interests) then, by all means, proceed. The effective negotiator is one who is able to predict the behavior of others. Therefore, if possible, the negotiator's behavior should be designed to enhance his or her ability to predict. What is perceived to be unpredictable behavior on your part usually creates unpredictable behavior on someone else's part. And that "someone else" could even be on your side of the table.

Exchanging Promises

As will be expressed throughout this book, the essence of the negotiating process, in any culture, over any issue, by any parties, is that it is an opportunity to exchange promises and commitments through which the parties will resolve problems and reach agreements. It is a very humanistic process. Therefore, the "give and take" of a negotiation is, for all intents and purposes, the actual exchange of promises.

Enhancing Implementation

While the essence of the negotiating process involves the actual exchange of promises and commitments, it is the keeping of said promises and commitments that is critical to maintaining the relationship. A positive relationship maintained through the close of the bargaining will help to insure the keeping of the promises. A negative relationship, which is created when the "lion shoves the deal down the lamb's throat," will usually result when promises are misunderstood, when commitments are half kept, or when misapplications or misinterpretations of the agreement are made. The above negative interaction obviously works against the maintenance of a positive relationship, making it even more difficult for the parties to engage in managing change and problem solving through the relationship. A forced deal usually results in passive-aggressive behavior.

Enhancing Enforcement

A positive relationship will usually yield a high-quality future dispute resolution clause such as one providing for mediation and/or arbitration. A positive relationship not only allows the parties an opportunity to focus on their immediate problems, but also should enable them to think rationally about potential future problems and anticipate changes so that they can co-design a future dispute resolution system. Hard work might be expended during the bargaining process to enhance a positive relationship, but it will be well worth the energy if enforcement problems are anticipated and dealt with through the co-design of a future dispute settlement system such as arbitration.

An advocate might also ask what other types of information and behavior are used to convince and persuade in a negotiation. Why do many advocates in a negotiation act in such hostile, intimidating ways? How does one negotiate with the other party to stipulate an issue or a fact when proceeding to an evidentiary (win/lose) hearing? Why take this approach when it is most useful in a negotiation to persuade the other side to become an advocate for one's own position to the other's closers/clients? How do we convince advocates who process information in a different way than we do? Shouldn't advocates know how mediators work and when they can be useful to a negotiation? What is the mind-set of the mediator in a negotiation? What do mediators take into consideration to help advocates reach settlement? How do we harness stress?

These and other concepts and questions will be discussed in this book. Please read on.

PART I

Approaching the Negotiation Process

Fundamentally, negotiation is a decision-making process. Through negotiation, we decide how to handle our differences in power, resources, perceptions, needs, interests, wants, facts, personalities, expectations, assumptions and values. We frequently clash over our differences and learn how to deal with them by watching our parents, teachers, schoolmates and cultural heroes in action. For instance, we have an idea of what happens in a courtroom because we've seen Perry Mason on TV. We have an idea of what happens between labor and management during collective bargaining because we've seen strike footage on the news. And we have an idea of how one buys an Oriental rug at a Middle Eastern bazaar because we've seen tourists and rug merchants haggling over prices in the movies.

Thus, when we find ourselves in negotiating situations, we act according to our perceptions of how one bargains. We reenact the models of behavior that we are familiar with to get what we want. And it frequently works against our own interests. Why? Because we may be using inappropriate models.

American society has often been called a litigious society. In the Washington, D.C., area alone there are 51,339 active members of the D.C. Bar Association as of February 2001 and over 200,000 cases are filed each year. At the first writing of this book, there were twice as many lawyers in Washington as there are in the entire country of Japan. In 1988, the United States graduated 10 lawyers for each engineer; Japan graduated 10 engineers for each lawyer. As of the writing of this second edition, the ratios have not changed significantly. Since an institution's importance in a culture (e.g., law, science, education, military, medicine, religion, sports, etc.) can be measured by the interest expressed in it by its populace, these statistics illustrate that the legal system in the United States clearly occupies a central place in our culture.

The typical legal model for dealing with disputes is an adversarial two-party process. At the adjudication stage it is win-lose. The plaintiff and defendant have a dispute, they present their two different sides in a court of law, and a judge decides between them. This adversarial model not only contributes to the perception of America as a litigious society, it also contributes to how we view the process of dispute resolution in general.

The irony, though, is that only about four percent of the cases filed for suit each year are actually adjudicated by a judge and jury. About 16 percent are dismissed, usually on procedural grounds, and approximately 80 percent are settled out of court through negotiation. Thus, the majority of cases filed for suit—80 percent—are decided through alternative means, and usually by lawyers.

When you add to this the many millions of commercial negotiations that take place daily in business and government—by lawyers, politicians, businesspeople, bankers, real estate agents, stock brokers, salespeople and their customers, insurance claims adjusters, labor-management professionals, legislators, lobbyists, etc.—we begin to look very much like a society of negotiators. In fact, rather than being a litigious society, we really are a negotiating society. Yet, as a society, we don't teach the process of negotiation with any degree of commitment. With a few exceptions, students can still get their law, business or government degrees without ever taking a course in negotiation. In fact, as of this writing, out of 185 law schools in the United States, a mere handful offer a course in negotiation and it is usually an elective. Thus, it is difficult for most people to be effective negotiators since they are neither educated in the negotiation process nor trained to negotiate.

When one considers that we value competition as a key motivator in our "can do" society, the situation worsens. In high schools, for example, we promote debating societies, not negotiating societies. From little league to professional sports, the win/lose model is advanced at every turn. The zero/sum principle—one wins to the extent that the other loses—is sincerely valued. However, the negotiating process is designed to end in a handshake—not in a winner over a loser.

The Basics of Negotiation

Even though negotiation is a decision-making process, we equate it with adversarial legal processes. This misconception about the process of negotiation stems from the cultural models of decision making that we pick up, and from the assumptions that we make based on those models we are familiar with, such as adjudication. Thus, many treat a negotiation as if it were a trial. There are fundamental differences between a trial, an administrative law proceeding or an arbitration and negotiation, even though they are all decision-making processes theoretically designed for closure. Let's take a closer look at some of these differences. Consider the following diagram representing four decision-making processes.

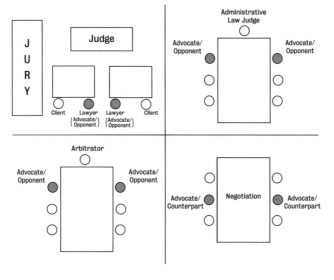

FIGURE 1

Figure 1 is a simplified diagram revealing the fundamental differences between the negotiating process and the other decision-making processes we have mentioned. The four questions below highlight the fundamental distinctions between negotiation and other processes:

(1) Who has the power to decide the outcome?
(2) Who wins and who loses?
(3) Who determines the "facts?"
(4) What is the essence of the process?

Question 1—who has the power to decide the outcome of a trial in a courtroom? The judge and/or jury.

Of an administrative law hearing? The administrative law judge.

Of an arbitration hearing? The arbitrator(s).

Of a two-party (bilateral) negotiation? Both parties decide the outcome of a bilateral negotiation. No one else. In your negotiations, who decides the outcome? You and your counterpart do together. The decision-making authority is not ceded to a third party. As long as it is a negotiation, the parties retain the decision-making power.

Question 2—who wins and who loses? In an adjudicatory setting, the judge, administrative law judge or arbitrator who decides the case determines that one side wins and one side loses. Period. The process is designed that way. In negotiation, there is a chance for an agreement with shared gains and, if the parties do not come to such an agreement, both sides might lose. When the parties come to an agreement, both sides win for the most part.[1]

Question 3—who determines the facts? In the courtroom, administrative law hearing and arbitration hearing, the judge, the administrative law judge and the arbitrator decide what the facts are and which are relevant. They are the deciders of facts (and of fate and remedy). In a negotiation the parties decide the facts (and fate and remedy). In a negotiation, however, as I noted previously, the facts are whatever both parties agree they are. If one side marshals a thousand pages of computer printouts with millions of numbers to support its position, and the other side does not agree to accept that information, it is not a fact for the purposes of that negotiation. Even if it is "true" by some objective outside standard. Conversely, if one side makes an assertion based on pure assumption and the statement is not challenged by the other side, then, for the purpose of that negotiation, it may become "fact." Even if it is not a fact by some objective outside standard.

Question 4—What is the essence of the process? The essence of adjudication is that it is a process designed to cede to a third-party decider of fact and fate the power and authority to decide disputes by selecting winners and losers according to proven fact, law and/or a contract. The essence of the negotiating process is that it provides an opportunity for the parties and/or disputants to exchange commitments and promises through which they can resolve their dispute and reach an agreement. The basic difference is that, in an adjudication process, the advocates attempt to create doubts in the mind of the neutral third party as to the viability of the other side's case, and in a negotiation the advocates attempt to create doubts in each other's minds as to the viability of their respective positions, interests, and expectations. This critical difference in the "target" for doubt creation will

---

1. The reason why it appears I am hedging on this point is that, even though there may be an agreement, not all participants on each side may feel they are winners. More on this point later.

be discussed in greater detail later as some advocates have difficulty shifting gears from a trial mind-set to a negotiating mind-set.

Negotiation is an ancient human process. Through this process, individuals and groups have historically addressed their differences at all levels—within and between different organizations, societies, states, nations, and civilizations. Over the centuries, we have placed many layers of "sophistication" on the negotiation process, but that does not change the essence of it. The negotiation process is anchored on your word and on their word—on what you promise to do or recommend in exchange for what they will promise to do or recommend.

In short, the negotiation process differs from the litigation, mediation, and arbitration processes in a number of ways, including who determines or controls the process design, the facts and information relevant to the case, and the outcome. To paraphrase the words of arbitrator/mediator Hart Hooper, with whom I have conducted many training seminars: "In *litigation*, the courts control the process and the courts control the outcome. In *arbitration*, the parties may control the design of the arbitration process, but the arbitrator controls the hearing and the outcome. In *mediation*, the mediator controls the process only with the permission of the parties, but the parties control the outcome. In *negotiation*, the parties control the process *and* the parties control the outcome."

So how should we conduct negotiations? How should we behave in a negotiation to get what we want? What we need? What we expect? Which "rules" or approaches should we follow? How do we manage behavior, expectations and resources? The following section covers five fundamental aspects of negotiation: (a) the first rule of negotiation; (b) the importance of the relationship; (c) the importance of trust; (d) the basic job of the negotiator; and (e) the management of expectations.

The Fundamentals of Negotiation

The principles discussed below will appear over and over again throughout this book. Please read them carefully so that you can better appreciate the interrelationship of these fundamental principles with the process and structure of negotiating.

The First Rule of Negotiation

The first rule of negotiation is that *there are no assumed rules for negotiation*. The absence of structure—the absence of "rules of negotiation"—is often the reason why many people are uncomfortable in the negotiation process. Most people know intuitively that if they are to be *convincing*, they need to be *confident*, and if they are to be confident, they need to be *com-*

fortable (comfortable, confident, and convincing are what I term the three C's of negotiation). Therefore, to make the process comfortable, the parties must negotiate the rules of engagement just like everything else, and these rules will be different for each negotiation.

Negotiating rules of engagement provides a way of working out your fears of negotiating. Our fears of the unknown, our fears of surprises, our fears of the unpredictable—they all work against our confidence and our ability to be our convincing best. Agreements regarding ground rules between parties are needed on essential issues such as time, place, duration, participants, scope of the formal discussions and agenda, as well as on seemingly trivial concerns such as the shape of the table. So, make the most of this opportunity. If you fear the other party will not keep important matters confidential, then negotiate a confidentiality understanding. If you fear the other side (or your own side) will "run to the media" with information, then a news blackout rule is appropriate. If you fear the other side may interrupt too much, then a rule on non-interruption is appropriate. In effect, such discussions are themselves preliminary negotiations which set the pace for the "substantive" negotiation to follow, and are just as critical as the substance of the negotiation.

Successful negotiation of even seemingly trivial concerns is essential to the eventual outcome of any negotiation because it is during the preliminary process, or "ground rule negotiations," that each side literally trains the other side as to how it negotiates. For instance, if members of the other side demand a round table at the beginning of every meeting during the preliminary series of talks, and we counter with a non-negotiable demand for a triangular table, but after three weeks of pushing we reluctantly agree to a round table, they have learned that we might not maintain over the long haul what appears to be a resolute position. They've learned that, if they push us for three weeks on a procedural matter, we'll knuckle under. Such discussions also give information to the other side about our intentions, the way we do business, or our patience, sincerity and reliability. In other words, they may begin to believe that our resolute position regarding a substantive issue may also waiver over time. The problem is they may be wrong. We may not yield. But the message we sent during the negotiation over process (the shape of the table) created an opportunity for them to miscalculate the firmness of our position.

The lessons learned will carry over from process negotiations to substantive negotiations. This can lead to miscalculation, impasse and failed negotiation if one side is resolute on a particular substantive issue, but has submitted to the other side's wishes regarding process issues during the course of the negotiation. The party giving a double or "mixed" message, engenders confusion. That party will appear to be inconsistent, wishy-washy and unreliable to the other side. To be an effective negotiator, you should be consistent in your negotiations of substantive as well as process concerns early in the negotiation—if you mean NO...SAY NO! If you mean MAYBE....SAY MAYBE! If you mean YES...SAY MAYBE! (There is usually time and opportunity to move from maybe to yes when the remainder of the deal satisfies your expectations.)

The Importance of the Relationship

As the preface to this book attempts to make clear, the relationship between parties in the negotiation is critically important. If the relationship between the parties is positive, actual negotiations should progress easily. A negative relationship between the parties will undoubtedly lead to very difficult negotiations. The more difficult the substantive issues, the more essential the positive relationship.

Developing a positive relationship may require examination of the values of the parties involved. For example, a series of training tapes developed for the Foreign Service Institute of the U.S. State Department depicts a mayor of a small village of a developing nation attempting to deal with Americans on various issues. The sequences include actors playing the roles of different Americans: a male state department official, a male military officer, a female Peace Corps volunteer, and an American businessman.

Regardless of the issue at hand, the tapes deliver a similar message: the mayor and the Americans are operating from different sets of values and cultural assumptions about how to get things done, about good working relationships, and about the meaning of time and status.

The Americans in the videos are constantly attempting to discuss the engineering or the technical aspects of "the problem." "The elevation of the roadbed is going to be this high. We're going to have this many bulldozers, trucks, and scrapers. Here's how we're going to operate our security system." And so on. The mayor in the videos is operating from a different framework, with different perspectives, assumptions, and values. He asks (when he can politely interrupt) "What part of the United States are you from? Where did you go to school? Are you married? How many children do you have?" He wants to understand the person with whom he is dealing.

The "problem" for the Americans is technical. The "problem" for the mayor is personal—the problem for the mayor is the relationship. When the relationship is strong, the mayor feels that "mere" technical difficulties in the future can be easily overcome through mutual agreement or through a subsequent negotiation. So the mayor wants to know who the person is. Why? Because if he doesn't know the other person, he can't trust him. If he can't learn to trust him, he won't take a risk with him. The mayor also wants a harmonious relationship for an emotional reason. Part of the reason is that positive and harmonious relationships are generally more pleasant to have than negative ones. But the mayor has a hardheaded or pragmatic reason, too. He wants to establish a long-term relationship. The relationship is the investment he is willing to make to ensure that things run smoothly for a long time to come during the implementation stage. Regardless of what technical problems come and go, the relationship will be constant over time, and the mayor wants to be able to depend on his American counterparts to keep their word. He wonders, are Americans dependable? He has heard many, many times from both his friends and enemies that Americans present themselves as responsible during the negotiation but do not appear to be very dependable during implementation. People from cultures where dependability is important do not like to take a risk with those whom they do not trust. We must remember that Americans, under the American value system and mind-set, assume that, if problems occur in the implementation stage of the agreement, a third party may be the decider of fact and fate who will choose a winner and loser if push comes to shove in the dispute. The mayor's mind-set is quite different. If "push comes to shove" in the mayor's mind, the parties will decide how to handle the problem. In other words, another negotiation will ensue and the mayor wants to be certain about his negotiating partner. Thus, at the point of a handshake, while the Americans think of this as the end of the negotiation, the mayor sees the handshake as just the beginning. The mayor knows that there is no such thing as a flawless agreement. We in the West want to rely on the written word as a way to maintain our rights while people of many other cultures rely on the relationship.

The Importance of Trust

If my team agrees with you, with your reasoning about the negotiation, it's just a matter of handing us a pen and simply saying, "Sign here," but usually it's not so easy. Usually there are difficult parts to a negotiation. If we get to the impasse-producing parts of a negotiation, and we do not trust each other, a deal is unlikely. But if we get to the difficult parts, and trust is built into the relationship, we have a better chance of coming to an agreement—one that benefits both of us.

The most effective negotiators are those who continually analyze the degree of trust in a given situation. An analysis of the trust in a relationship is a much better predictor of how well the negotiation will turn out than volumes of technical data supporting a position. We should then spend time and resources analyzing, developing and maintaining trust; it determines the success or failure of our negotiations.

By trust, I do not necessarily mean some fuzzy kind of feeling that leaves us vulnerable to the exploitation of others. I mean being able to rely on the other party's behavior and to be counted on by it in turn. This kind of trust derives from one's reliability and leads directly to credibility. Let's illustrate with a worst-case scenario.

Suppose you are called in to negotiate after someone else has made a "botch" of it. How do you establish trust? How do you fix it? Do you do it with a nice speech about the importance of trust? Not necessarily. You do it with small transactions, with modest demonstrations of reliability, and by being perceived as dependable and trustworthy.

Create a history of reliability. If you say, "I'll call you at 12:37 p.m.," call at 12:37 p.m. If you say, "I'll have our proposal to you by 9:00 a.m. tomorrow morning," have the proposal on the person's desk by 9:00 a.m. But beware about letting the other party tell you how to be reliable. Remember, you pick the methods of reliability, and then demonstrate your reliability convincingly. You must establish a sequence of "microtrust transactions" to establish the "macrotrust" necessary for a solid relationship.

"Build Mutual Trust First, Then Talk Turkey" was a caption in the *Christian Science Monitor* years ago under a picture of Turkish Prime Minister Turgut Ozal. The accompanying article spoke of attempts by the government of Greece and Turkey to address centuries'-old differences between the two states: "Turkish officials say Ozal will give priority to 'confidence-building' measures. Ozal was expected to present to the Greek Prime Minister a package of suggestions on ways to build mutual trust, including trade, economic cooperation, tourism, cultural exchanges, and revision of school history books." This is how Turkey and Greece are attempting to build a positive relationship. The same process of building trust operates in any negotiation relationship.

"Do you hear what I hear?"
Bing Crosby

Communication. Because the essence of the negotiation process is that it is an exchange of promises and commitments, we won't accept someone else's promise or commitment if we do not trust the other party or the people whom they represent, and vice versa. Additionally, when trust is low or nonexistent in a relationship, the parties find it difficult to communicate with each other. When communication is problematic in a relationship, parties do not listen effectively to each other as each states its expectations, problems, interests, wants, needs, alternative solutions, demands and proposals or counterproposals and its rationale for any of the above. Ineffective listening due to poor communication because of low trust levels actually creates additional problems in understanding and trust. A vicious cycle, indeed. This is why any negotiation is essentially defined by the trust in the relationship among the parties. The greater the need for risk taking in a negotiation, the greater the need for a trusting relationship because *people do not take great risks or communicate effectively with others whom they do not trust.*

Education. If our relationship is a positive one, if we can depend on each other and if our word is credible to each other and our communication is good, then the chances are better that we can reach a mutually acceptable and beneficial agreement. When effective listening is absent or weak in a relationship, it is not possible for each side to educate the other as to the viability of its positions, interests and expectations. When we have a high degree of trust and confidence in our relationship, it's much easier to communicate, allowing negotiators to convince and persuade by educating each other. That kind of education is one of the most constructive activities of any negotiation.

Understanding expectations. An improved relationship will give rise to enhanced listening, which in turn will allow for better understanding of the expectations of the respective parties. A better understanding of expectations opens the door to more effective management of expectations.

Managing expectations. When education is allowed to occur within the context of negotiation, it is the most important way for the expectations of the negotiating parties to be understood, and, when necessary, managed or lowered. Understanding the equation between expectations and proposals is critical to the bargaining part of negotiation. If an expectation cannot be lowered, a proposal that fails to meet that expectation will either be rejected or accepted reluctantly, with the result that one can assume difficulties in the implementation of the agreement through passive-aggressive behavior. If the expectations can be learned and understood, an opportunity is afforded either to raise the proposal to meet that expectation or work to lower the expectation within the proposal range, or both. If expectations cannot be lowered for any reason, then, in order for a settlement to be reached, the proposal must be increased. Increasing proposals can cost dearly.

Stability. A related way to build trust is to make sure that the other party is never surprised—that is a key. You will destabilize the people you're working with by surprising them in any way, thus hurting any chance of a positive atmosphere in the negotiations. For every move you make, no matter how small or apparently insignificant, it is important to make certain there are no surprises unless you can predict with deadly accuracy the resulting implications of the surprise. Even "pleasant" surprises can have a destabilizing impact on the negotiations because others may then begin to question their own ability to predict, which could then lead to uncertainty and a limit in the amount of their risk taking.

Suppose you and the other side are just talking generally about the upcoming negotiation during the early stages of your relationship. If you agree to discuss certain items, arrive prepared to discuss those items. Don't say, "Gee, I'm sorry, I'm not prepared to discuss that item or issue," or "Gee, I have a few more items I'd like to put on today's agenda." As I indicated earlier, if you agree to the meeting at 10:30 a.m., you should be there, ready to begin by 10:30 a.m. Again, if you are going to be there at 10:40 a.m., call well in advance of 10:30 a.m. to make certain the other team knows you are going to be late. If you agree to bring Sally, Moe, Jack, and Curly, bring Sally, Moe, Jack, and Curly. If Curly gets sick, call the other team and explain, "Curly's not going to be with us. I'm going to substitute Frieda for Curly." It sounds simple, doesn't it? But too many people disturb the negotiating relationship by simply not keeping their word on what appear to be minor procedural matters and by surprising the other side.

Paying close attention to the relationship builds trust. Trust lessens resistance to risk taking inherent in a difficult negotiation, and provides the opportunity to communicate, educate, manage expectations, create doubts and uncertainties and exchange promises and commitments.

The Basic Job of a Negotiator

"You've got my mind messed up."
James Carr

The basic job of a negotiator is to create doubts and uncertainties in the minds of others as to the viability of their positions. An effective negotiator is a "doubt creator." He or she persuades, influences, and convinces the members of the other party to a negotiation to change their position. Negotiators must create trust and confidence in the minds of others to provide a basis for creating doubts and uncertainties. Creating doubts and uncertainties is critical to changing minds, which helps to change the other party's behavior, which affects its position, interests, and expectations. Negotiators who are not trusted will not be given the time of day, let alone the time and opportunity to allow doubts to be created. The creation of trust is a step-by-step process, as is the creation of doubts—enough time and opportunity is crucial for effective advocacy. Of course, the most effective way for negotiators to create trust and confidence, and, conversely, to create doubts in the minds of the parties, is to be themselves. Creating trust is essential to the creation of doubts!

For example, let's say we disagree about something. You, as a negotiator, want a behavioral change in me. Before I change my behavior, you have to change my mind-set. And before I change my mind-set, I have to doubt what it is that I believe. Conversely, I am not going to change your behavior unless you first change the way you think about something. And you're not going to change the way you think until you first doubt what you believe. In short, if you don't agree with me about something, then my job is to create a doubt in your mind as to the viability of your position, and vice versa. For example, the lead negotiator would create doubts and uncertainties with the stabilizers on his or her team by suggesting that the principal/closer/client/ratifier will not accept such a weak settlement. With one's destabilizers, the lead negotiator would talk about the costs of nonsettlement.

You really cannot create doubts until you have someone's trust. This concept applies to your own team. Once again, that's one reason why we spend a lot of time building trust and confidence within our own team. Those on your negotiating team must be trained to think and act like a team. Training and teamwork are essential and they can be accomplished during planning and during caucuses.

Managing Their Expectations

We are often told by professional negotiators that we should raise our aspiration level in negotiation—that we should raise and maintain our expectations. That's only half of the story. We spend entirely too much time on what we expect, and not enough time on what the other side expects. We spend too much time in negotiations thinking about our approach, positions, problems, goal, strategy, objectives, appropriate tactics to meet those objectives, team discipline, making sure that we have the correct resources delivered at the appropriate times, etc.

We don't spend enough time in any given negotiation understanding what the other party's expectations are. It is only with that understanding, however, that we can begin to manage our counterparts' expectations. Why? Because it is necessary to manage the expectations of the other party as to the eventual outcome, as well as about our ability to deliver. Why? Because we want satisfaction, and we want the members of the other side to be satisfied. If they're not expecting much and they get "something in excess of what they expect," they will be satisfied. If they expect a great deal and get "something less," they will be dissatisfied, and stand poised to reject your offer. Knowing their expectations and then lowering their expectations about the ultimate outcome of the negotiations is essential. Our ratifiers may also on occasion have unrealistic expectations and you may need to manage their expectations as well.

Expectation management should begin very early. Let's imagine we are beginning a commercial negotiation with the heads of another company. They think they can profit by one million dollars dealing with us. But, by managing their expectations, we may convince them that they will be fortunate if they make five hundred thousand dollars. Thus, they will be delighted to receive seven hundred thousand dollars in profit! And they will "like" us for it, rather than resent us. However, if we had asked them to settle for seven hundred thousand, but they believed they could have received one million (because we had not effectively managed their expectations), the relationship may well have been spoiled, they may well have perceived that we had taken advantage of them, and future dealings may become unlikely.

Similarly, lowering your counterparts' expectations about you will help, too. Be modest. Play yourself down. If you try to impress them with your flash, your brilliance, your incredible sense of humor and your wealth, you are probably working against your own interests. They will tend to think of you as a smart, tough opponent, and they may act defensively, raise their barriers and perhaps prepare themselves for a battle with you. You will then have to work even harder to lower the barriers that you really helped to create. If you behave in a low-key, relaxed, even dull manner, they will tend to think of you as conciliatory, perhaps even as an "easy mark" and they may let their barriers down. (Albeit very exaggerated, TV's Columbo personifies this behavior.)

We must manage our counterparts' expectations first by knowing them, then by understanding them, and then by creating doubts in their minds when we need to manage those expectations. Once managed, the key to settlement is not the satisfaction of wants, needs, and hopes, but the satisfaction of expectations.

How do we manage expectations by creating those doubts? We must educate ourselves about our counterparts' positions, interests and expectations by listening and observing. They'll help us do it; they'll even appreciate us for taking the time to listen. We must ask appropriate questions and listen to their responses. Second, we must look behind their positions and interests in order to understand their real problems, perceptions, assumptions, values and expectations. Third, and this is most critical, we must look for the seeds of doubt they may have in their own expectations, perceptions and assumptions.

Fundamentals of the Process

"You must remember this, a kiss is just a kiss."
—from the movie "Casablanca"

And a position is only a position. Every position is based on a series of assumptions, and every assumption contains its own seed of doubt. In a negotiation, announcing an initial position is usually the first crude attempt to affect the expectations of the other side. No experienced negotiator in our Western society arrives at a negotiation table assuming that his or her initial position will be wholeheartedly accepted by the other party. Our counterparts may come with the assumption that theirs' is a reasonable proposal, but they know that they need information to be certain. It is part of their job to get information from you. It is part of your job to get information from them—to educate yourself about their needs, to let them know what you need, to create doubts in their minds about their initial position, and to lower their expectations about the ultimate outcome. You know what you know. The object of creating and maintaining a positive relationship is to use the actual negotiation process as a discovery process to find out what they know. In a negotiation, knowledge and information are power.

An assumption is only an assumption. As noted earlier, every assumption contains its own seed of doubt. Listen. You will hear your counterparts' underlying assumptions. They will share them with you. Whether they know you personally or not, they carry assumptions about you because of the identity groups to which you and they belong—assumptions about Americans; about males and females; about whites, blacks, Hispanics, Asians and Middle Easterners; about people in business, white collars, blue collars, pink collars; in law, in the military or in government service. Listen carefully for these underlying assumptions. These assumptions contain seeds of doubt. For those assumptions which are considered negative, act in a way that is inconsistent with them if acting in such a way enhances your interest and still allows you to be yourself. For those assumptions which are positive and support your cause, act in accordance with them. Energize their doubts about their own initial assumptions if their initial assumptions work against your best interests. Their assumptions about you will also give you information about their values.

Negotiators create facts and nonfacts. In negotiation, an unchallenged assumption usually becomes a "fact" for that particular negotiation. In an evidentiary procedure setting, the basic job of an attorney or a nonlawyer advocate in arbitration is to create doubts in the mind of the *third-party deciders of fact*—the arbitrator, adjudication panel, judge, administrative law judge, jury—as to the viability of the other advocate's position or theory of the case beyond whatever quantum of proof is appropriate. In an evidentiary procedure, the advocate is limited to supporting his or her theory by eliciting facts supported by evidence that the advocate hopes the third-party decider of fact will accept as proof of the facts alleged.

As I have indicated earlier, in the negotiation process, *the deciders of fact* sit across the table from each other. While evidentiary procedures are oriented to facts and to establishing "the truth of the matter," in the negotiation process the "truth of the matter" is whatever the negotiators agree it is. Negotiators may take scientifically/legally/historically provable facts and, by agreement, render them "nonfacts" if "the facts" create problems for the negotiators as they attempt to settle their dispute. Further, if negotiators disagree among themselves as to what constitutes fact, then, in that negotiation, the "fact" is not a fact because of the disagreement. Since many disciplines rely on facts for decision making, the consternation and frustration by individuals who base decision making on scientifically, technically, and legally created logic is understandable. In a negotiation, decisions are reached not so much on legal, technical, scientific or historical grounds as generally understood, but rather on "facts" as the negotiators understand and perceive them and as the negotiators agree as to what information is "fact." Further, when professional negotiators negotiate, they do not conduct a trial. They usually make an assertion based on an assumption with only some degree of certainty. Hearing no objection, the assertion may be accepted as fact. It is usually when a third-party decision-making process is closing in (the courthouse steps or the arbitration hearing date) that the negotiator wonders whether assertions made in a settlement negotiation can be proven with appropriate evidence in an evidentiary hearing. Thus valuable time and resources can be wasted in trying to determine whether or not to accept a settlement offer if parties are not continually assessing the viability of information asserted as fact.

Values are fundamental to a person's identity. There are two problems with attempting to change another's values—one is ethical and the other is practical. In the process of building a relationship and negotiating with others, you will learn a great deal about where people's values lie. Values are critical to who a person is, and how each person fits into and defines his or her world.

I have made a personal choice not to attempt to alter people's values, even if I thought I could. I believe that the ethical targets for creating doubt are the other side's positions, perceptions, and assumptions that affect its expectations. That's an educational process. I do not choose to target fundamental values for doubt creation; others may.

In addition to ethical constraints, the practical problem with changing another's values is that it is extremely difficult. The more central and culturally bound the values, the more difficult to change. Psychiatrists have difficulty changing the values of people who want to change. You may be dealing with people who don't want to change. If a negotiation is important, it is likely stressful. People who begin to feel more and more insecure as stress increases, are more likely to reaffirm their values than to change them. The probability of success in modification of values in that instance is relatively small. Even if you could change someone's values, and that person returned to "sell" the deal to his or her ratifiers who realized that their negotiators had turned their backs on their own values, would they accept the deal? Probably not. You really don't want to make the other party your clone. You want the other party's members to become your advocates and to agree with you for their own reasons in order to maintain credibility with the people who sent them to the negotiating table.

You might, however, be dealing with others who are quite interested in changing your values. Keep in mind that your values are derived from the groups and subcultures to which you belong, and if you are not clear about what values are central to you, or whom you represent and are not "well-centered," you leave yourself open to having them changed. Should others change your values significantly, you may be making the future difficult for yourself and with those whom you represent. Being forewarned is being forearmed.

Below is a hierarchy of practical and psychological levels on which we operate in a negotiation. In a negotiation, you should probe for the seeds of doubt in your counterparts' positions, their definition of the problem, their perception and their assumptions. You should also become familiar with their expectations, fundamental values and interests, and treat them with respect.

Position (on an issue)
Problem (creating the position)
Interests (also creating the position)
Perceptions (of the problem)
Expectations (satisfaction level)
Assumptions (underlying the problem)
Values (underlying the assumptions)

Privacy is important. Since negotiators rely on their personal perceptions and understandings with their opposites to establish an agreement, they have a profound need for privacy. As I indicated earlier, nearly 80 percent of cases filed for suit in the United States are not adjudicated by a judge and jury, but are settled out of court through negotiation without unnecessary public disclosure. The existence of millions of voluntarily negotiated arbitration clauses, which, by their very existence, energize the negotiation process, further supports this phenomenon. The large number of grievance settlements in labor relations and the large number of insurance claims adjusted through negotiation, voluntary mediation, arbitration and the many domestic and international political and commercial negotiations, also underscores not only the frequency of private settlement, but also the importance of privacy in the creation of these settlements.

Since privacy is such a critical and essential characteristic of the negotiation process, the actual events during a high-stakes negotiation are seldom known, either during or after the negotiation. The only available information is whatever the negotiators choose to reveal. Many times the negotiators themselves are unaware of all that has happened in terms of implications until time has passed.

Summary

To summarize what I have discussed in Part I:

—The First Rule of Negotiation is that there are no assumed rules for negotiation—you must first negotiate them.

—The Essence of Negotiation is that it provides an opportunity for parties to a dispute to exchange commitments and promises.

—The Relationship between the parties is the most critical variable in determining the climate and the ultimate outcome of a negotiation.

—Trust is the central issue of a relationship. No party to a negotiation will take risks by having its mind changed without some degree of trust.

—The Basic Job of a negotiator is to create doubts in the minds of your counterparts as to the viability of their positions. Listen to what they are trying to communicate. Learn their positions, interests, perspectives, perceptions, assumptions, expectations, and values. Then work to create doubts in their minds when appropriate.

—Manage Their Expectations. Begin to lower their expectations early in the negotiation. Later, should they begin to lose hope that an agreement can be reached, you may need to raise their expectations to convince them that an agreement is possible.

In Part I, I have given you a picture of how we typically approach the negotiation process. I have said that our ideas about negotiation are derived from cultural assumptions which cast a basic decision-making process in a win/lose adversarial situation. While some negotiations may include aspects of conflict, I have characterized the process of negotiation not as an adversarial process, but as a joint decision-making process. The essence of negotiation is broader than the resolution of conflict; it involves an exchange of promises and commitments. This exchange is a fundamental pattern of human interaction and requires a degree of trust.

In the next section, I'll present an extended model, a "multidimensional" configuration of the negotiation process, that will help you understand the process as it occurs, not just as a two-party model, but, in many cases, as a multiparty, multidimensional transaction. In addition, I will attempt to convince the reader that the negotiator has more power and flexibility by not having the authority to ratify the deal and that the processes of negotiation and ratification should be kept separate, with the ratifier not appearing at the table except for mutually agreed-upon ceremonial reasons.

PART II

The Structure of Negotiation

"In negotiations, you don't get what you want—you get what you negotiate."
—Chester Karras

"What you see is what you get."
—Flip Wilson

"What you don't see is better yet."
—Tina Turner

"What you get is what you perceive you got."
—Arthur E. Berkeley

"In negotiations, you get what you expect to get."
—Thomas R. Colosi

"What you see is not necessarily what you get."
—Thomas R. Colosi

The important concepts of the negotiation process that have been mentioned—the exchange of promises, the development of trust, the creation of doubt, the management of expectations—occur within the framework of either an informal or formal structure of relationships. These relationships occur within organizational and institutional frameworks, and form the foundations and structural dimensions of any negotiation.

The Structure of Negotiation

When a negotiation such as arms control or collective bargaining is reported in the mass media, the press usually depicts the negotiation as a meeting of basically two undifferentiated sides sitting across a table from each other. A reporter might describe the situation by commenting, "The Americans and the Soviets sat down again today in Geneva," or "The United Auto Workers and Chrysler have suspended their contract talks for an indefinite period."

This description oversimplifies the negotiation process and portrays its structure as a one-dimensional/two-party process that occurs only when the media states it is occurring. Negotiation is said to be "bilateral" when there are two parties engaged in discussions. The negotiation is often represented—perhaps misrepresented—as a bargaining transaction between two entities: two individuals, such as a husband and wife, salesman and shopper, teacher and student, boss and subordinate; or else two groups such as arms-control delegations from the former Soviet Union and United States, congressional conferences of Republicans and Democrats, negotiating teams from Congress and the White House, commercial teams from Xerox and Fujitsu or collective bargaining teams from labor and management.

This simplistic portrayal overlooks the multidimensional structure of the negotiation process. While most negotiations are portrayed as two-party affairs, there are really several basic dimensions: (1) the horizontal (H) negotiations with the other team, (2) the internal (I) negotiations within your own team, and (3) the ratification (R) negotiations between you and your organizational hierarchy and the negotiations that occur within your organizational hierarchy or ratification group and theirs. Successful negotiators have learned to manage or attempt to manage the expectations and the relationships among all of these dimensions.

The Horizontal Dimension (H)

The horizontal dimension is the one you see on TV and read about in the newspapers. It is also the dimension you experience when you are negotiating with a salesperson for a new car. It is the face-to-face interaction with the "other side" and often takes place across a table or desk. The horizontal dimension is the most visible stage on which the negotiation drama unfolds, and it is quite often a formal and highly stylized performance with a high degree of role-playing. Misunderstanding the negotiation process begins with misunderstanding the horizontal dimension.

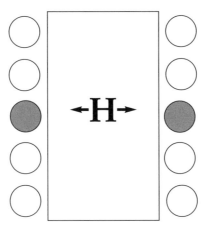

FIGURE 2

Figure 2 illustrates the horizontal dimension of a typical bilateral negotiation. "H" stands for horizontal dimension of the core structural model of negotiation. The horizontal dimension is an important dimension of the negotiation process, but not for commonly understood reasons. The inexperienced negotiator or onlooker perceives a great deal of negotiating and bargaining occurring across the table. The experienced negotiator sees that, too, but also much more.

Most people believe the substantive work of negotiation is done at the table. This is not necessarily true. If the negotiations have been handled well by both sides, the difficult substantive work is conducted off the record, away from the table such as discussions in the hallway or over the phone with a representative from the other side, internal discussions back in the hotel within your own team (I=internal dimension), and horse trading among departments within your own organizational hierarchy (R=ratification dimension). These are the dimensions where many tough key decisions are made about how many units—be they warheads, wages or widgets—can be "delivered" or "not delivered" to the other side at the table during the horizontal negotiation process. In a complex negotiation, the work that actually gets done at the table is largely concerned with defining the "rules" and process of that particular negotiation and playing out an agreed upon schedule.

Education. If the atmosphere and the relationship is positive, the horizontal dimension offers a forum for educating the other side in obvious and not so obvious ways. Formally, both sides use this dimension to exhibit their proposals, computer printouts, and experts. Informally, both sides, depending on the degree of sophistication, attempt to co-define the mutually acceptable "rules" of negotiation. During these contact hours you might "tip each other off" as to how each side "does business": Are you trustworthy? Are you considerate? Are you dignified? Are you impatient? Can you be intimidated? Are you rigid and dogmatic or are you solid and reasonable? How about the other side?

The horizontal dimension provides a stage for both sides to perform. This permits the two sides to define the general tenor of the negotiations. If the relationship between parties is positive and cordial, the parties may use horizontal interactions to provide introductions, positive speeches, and the offering of well-prepared and effectively reasoned proposals with underlying interests explained to the fullest. If the relationship between the parties is not particularly cordial and the atmosphere remains negative, the parties use horizontal interaction to stage angry accusations, insults, and the presentation of nonnegotiable demands. This is usually a waste of time, money, and resources.

When you negotiate, the people sitting across the table from you are not a monolithic group. Even though you may perceive them as unified, their team is composed of individuals just as yours. Their individuality gives an internal structure to their team. Experienced negotiators know that each team has both a formal and an informal internal structure, and they strive to understand it. This team structure can be depicted as the internal dimension of a negotiation. Effective negotiators have learned to manage both teams along the horizontal dimension and the internal dimension.

The Internal Dimension (I)

When members of one team look across the table at members of another team, they tend to see an undifferentiated collection of people with shared and uniform attributes. This is a false perception that can lead to trouble.

As previously noted, no team is a monolith. Yours isn't. Theirs isn't. Their team may look like a monolith, walk like a monolith and talk like a monolith—that's because its members appear to be alike, and they may have been instructed to act in that manner in order to appear unified—but they are not a monolith. For tactical reasons, each team seeks to appear harmonious to outsiders. You know that your team isn't a monolith—you've been working with it for some time. You discovered at the first meeting with your team that there are fundamental differences among its members. Differences among team members are present in the internal dimension of any negotiation team.

Within any team, members hold different attitudes and—consciously and unconsciously—play different roles. The internal structure of each team may include three subsets of team members—the stabilizers (S), the destabilizers (DS) and the chief spokesperson(s), or quasi-mediator(s)

(QM). Negotiators typically fall into three subsets of team members. These three subsets are depicted in Figure 3.

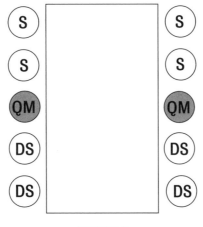

FIGURE 3

Figure 4 on the following page depicts two negotiating teams as they might appear at the table. "I" stands for the internal dimension of the core structural model of negotiation. Who on your team are the stabilizers, destabilizers and quasi-mediators? How do you tell them apart? They'll tell you. All you have to do is listen patiently to what they say, and watch their nonverbal behavior. This, of course, is also true in understanding the internal structure and dynamics of the other side. Stabilizers and destabilizers are sometimes purposefully selected. Sometimes you may have little control over their appearance on the team, but it is important to know where they are coming from in terms of attitude. I'll exaggerate each subset to emphasize the potential problematic behavior.

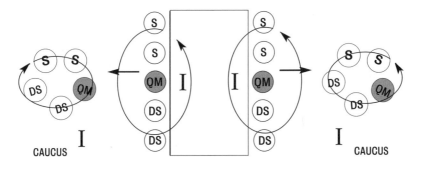

FIGURE 4

The stabilizers (S). The stabilizers on your team are easy to recognize. Everyone has known and worked with stabilizers in school, at the office, and in the shop. They're the "nice people" on your team. The stabilizer sees the negotiation process as stabilizing. A stabilizer sees negotiation as a way to avoid war, a court battle or a strike; they tend to be averse to conflict. They say things such as, "We're all just the same at heart" and "Why can't we just be friends?" Stabilizers demand little and offer much. They tend to be what authors Roger Fisher and Bill Ury, in their book *Getting To Yes*, call "soft" negotiators—soft on the people and soft on the issues. If left alone, in a worst-case scenario, stabilizers may get "taken to the cleaners" by the other side.

Stabilizers tend to trust others, even when the trust isn't warranted. Stabilizers demonstrate their agreeability with their words and with their deeds. They also demonstrate their agreeability with their body language by frequently nodding their heads. They usually fall into line when authority is applied, regardless of which side applies it. They are easy for you to work with, and they are easy for the other side to work with. This is not necessarily an advantage for either side unless the stabilizers on a team can be managed.

The destabilizers (DS). The destabilizers on your team are even easier to recognize than the stabilizers. They are more verbal. You've probably been having trouble with them from day one. In a worst-case scenario, they don't like the negotiation process. They don't trust the negotiation process. They think it's a waste of time. They don't like the other team. They think their own team should be back home, doing something more constructive such as preparing for a strike, or preparing for a war, or preparing a case for trial. They may not like or trust you. Destabilizers are generally not conflict averse; they may even like it. They say things such as, "It's a dog-eat-dog world" and, "Do unto others before they do unto you." Destabilizers drive hard bargains. They tend to be what Fisher and Ury call "hard" negotiators—hard on the people and hard on the issues. This is not necessarily a disadvantage for either side if the destabilizers on a team can be managed.

Destabilizers tend to mistrust the other side and those on their own team who want to negotiate a deal. They tend to see their stabilizers and their team spokesperson as "patsies," who will unwittingly "give away the store." Destabilizers frequently resist authority—anyone's authority, and they don't listen very well to anyone else's point of view. If left alone, destabilizers can overpower, intimidate, create mistrust and ultimately sabotage the internal relationship on the team, the horizontal relationship across the table, and the entire negotiation process.

A military officer who is a stabilizer might sacrifice long-term security for a short-term cease-fire. A military officer who is a destabilizer might sacrifice a rapprochement with an adversary because he sees it as a trick or as detrimental to long-term security. Thus, he may unconsciously make a conflict inevitable that he consciously sought to avoid.

Within a team where destabilizers want to fight and stabilizers want to make friends, someone hopefully is in charge. This is usually the formally designated head, or "lead" negotiator or team spokesperson. Stabilizers tend to see their destabilizers and the team spokesperson as being too hard on the other team, jeopardizing a possible deal. If your team spokesperson or team chief is a stabilizer, that person may do everything possible, including using the leverage from the stabilizers, to make a deal at any cost.

If your team chief is a destabilizer, that person may do everything to sabotage a deal, including using the leverage from the destabilizers. So you may never reach agreement—on your team, with your organization or with the other side. Usually, if an organization is interested in coming to an agreement and understands the negotiation process, it sends a quasi-mediator type to the table as head of the negotiating team.

The quasi-mediator (QM). In the present core structural model, I label the head of a negotiation team as the QM, or Quasi-Mediator. To be an effective lead negotiator, you must not only effectively manage the relationship "across the table" between your team and the other team—the horizontal dimension (H) (the dimension on which many negotiation text books concentrate)—but you must manage your own team, and you must manage the interaction between the team across the table and those who send you to the table to represent their interests.

The QM perhaps tends to be what Fisher and Ury refer to as a "principled negotiator"—soft on the people and hard on the issues. The QM orchestrates the negotiation process, and usually fully understands the process. One of the QM's biggest jobs is managing his or her own team's expectations, their ratifier, and the expectations of those across the table.

As you sit in the seat of a team spokesperson or team chief during countless negotiations, you gain experience, and realize that most of your time is spent "mediating" between the above subsets or factions on your own team.You use the same convincing and persuading skills heading a negotiating team that you would use in the role of a neutral mediator, except you have a particular point of view. Excellent negotiators are usually excellent mediators in this sense. A quasi-mediator, however, must not be confused with the role of the neutral mediator. The quasi-mediator is, like any negotiator, an advocate for the interests of his or her side. But in your role, as the head of your team or your delegation, you will find yourself negotiating (advocating), mediating (facilitating), and arbitrating (deciding) between the positions of the stabilizers and destabilizers on your own team, and interacting in a similar way between those whom you represent and those sitting across the table.

The Ratification Dimension (R)

Often, the internal negotiations are more contentious than the negotiations that occur across the table. No matter how well you manage the other team and your own team, however, you must, above all, effectively manage your relationship with those who have ratification authority—those who send you to the table. The "bottom line" of any negotiation is a line that is more than theoretically drawn by the people who sent you to the table to negotiate; those with the authority to close, the "closers" or the "ratifiers." This relationship is depicted by the ratification dimension (R) of the core structural model of negotiation.

The ratification dimension of a negotiation marks the relationship between your team and your organizational hierarchy and among departments of your organizational hierarchy. The ultimate decision about whether or not your team can "cut a deal" with the other team lies with the people who send you to the table. The opposite organizational ratification hierarchies may define and redefine the limits of any agreement that the two sides at the table attempt to reach.

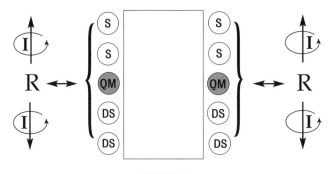

FIGURE 5

Figure 5 illustrates the ratification dimension of a typical bilateral negotiation. "R" stands for the ratification dimension of one's organizational hierarchy in the core structural model of negotiation.

The closer(s). The people (or person) who send you to the table to negotiate are also referred to as your closers. They have the power and authority to "close" the deal—to approve, to sign, and to "bless" any agreement. Very rarely should the closer come to the table. The negotiator will come to the table, but the closer will stay away—for some good reasons. As noted earlier, Abraham Lincoln said it best when he commented that "a lawyer who represents himself has a fool for a client." One assumes Lincoln was thinking of an advocate in a court trial. Since trial advocacy was less prevalent in those days, he probably meant that clients who have emotional attachments to substantive issues should use the service of a lawyer in a negotiation.

Another example—imagine you are interested in buying a new car. You do some homework, and you select a reputable dealership for one of the makes that interests you. You walk into the showroom to look at the new models—"Just browsing," you tell the salesperson, attempting to manage the expectations of the salesperson. Sooner or later, you begin asking prices. The salesperson responds, "That's the sticker price on the window (designed to manage your expectations), but I might be able to shave a little off for you. Make me a reasonable offer." Perhaps after making a low-ball offer and bargaining a bit for fun, you make what you consider to be a fair and reasonable offer. The salesperson pauses. He or she then leaves, presumably to discuss the reasonableness of your offer with the closer. In any event, the salesperson soon returns and says something such as: "Though of course I can see the reasonableness of your position, the manager has forbidden me from cutting such an exceptional deal. The manager feels we would be giving the car away at that price."

The way this negotiation is structured has a number of advantages for the dealership and is the reason why most dealerships use this model. Notice the salesperson is positioned between you and the "real" decision maker in the organizational hierarchy. The salesperson's "bread and butter" depends on how much money he or she can get from you, yet the person presumes to be your friend and attempts to become your representative with the hard-bargaining sales manager. Remarkable! The salesperson can use the manager to stall for time, offer alternative proposals ("But we have a 'cherry' of a used car out back that the manager says..."), and so on. The salesperson is thus protected from being forced to make quick, and possibly costly, decisions or promises to act. Perhaps most important, he or she can retain a cordial relationship with you by using the closer as a buffer. It may at first appear paradoxical, but, by virtue of the salesperson using an absent closer, he or she has seemingly reduced his or her personal power, yet in fact has obtained more power in the negotiation. Ah, if we can but quell our egos and admit we are "only the negotiator," how much more powerful would we be in a negotiation with an absent closer!

The salesperson's closer is in the back office, inaccessible to you. Where is your closer? The salesperson will try to find out. The salesperson may also try to hook your ego into the transaction by asking who makes the car-buying decisions in your family (In other words: "Who is the powerful person in your marriage or relationship, you or your spouse or significant other?"). The salesperson may ask you to bring your spouse in to look at the car when you "really" want to buy. This is a famous strategy in time-share condominium sales—both spouses (the negotiator and closer) must be present to get the promotion "prize." It may gratify your ego if you tell the salesperson that you have the power to make the decision right then and there, but then you will be bargaining at a disadvantage. Your apparent increase in personal power actually disempowers you to a great extent. If the agent is playing hardball, he or she will probably ask something like, "Can you make a commitment to me right here and now? Because if you can, I'll try to get you a price that you'll never see again after today (setting a deadline)." Normally, you would not want to take the bait, because it is generally in your best interest to have a closer away from the table to protect you—just as the salesperson has. It is important to note in this particular type of transaction that an emotional detachment between the negotiator and the ratifier is critical since emotions can cloud thinking and decision making.

I realize that this advice may be counterintuitive. As long as we perceive the negotiation process as confrontational and adversarial, we want all the armament we can muster. We really believe that being both the negotiator and the ratifier/closer gives us that power. The salesperson (as negotiator) only promises to recommend something to the sales manager (as ratifier) while we, as customers (negotiator/ratifiers), promise to act. Leverage goes to the dealership since the salesperson can still keep the promise to recommend while the sales manager may choose not to act.

There may be rare times, however, when you want your closer(s) at the table. You may, for example, want your closer there at both the initial and final ceremonial meetings to underline the importance of the negotiation, to add credibility to your authority to negotiate if it is in question, or to lend sincerity to your protests. This should be done only as part of a conscious strategy, and only within the context of any particular negotiation. In general, keep your closer away. It gives you more room to maneuver, more flexibility, and, in certain cases, it may make it easier on your relationship with the other side. It empowers you to openly admit to the other side's members that you are just the negotiator. As long as they believe you have the ability to effectively recommend, you still have power.

The ratification negotiation. The negotiation between your team and its closers—the people from your organization's vertical hierarchy who sent you to the table—usually begins, unfortunately, in a reactive way since little proactive planning precedes many negotiations. Your team, after some time at the table, around the table and in private informal meetings with the other side, is becoming more and more convinced and persuaded by some of your counterpart team's approaches. You have discussed the issues horizontally with the other team and internally among yourselves, and you begin to entertain the idea of modifying your position. Can you make a counterproposal? If the change in your position is significant, you must first check with your closers.

You meet with your closers and you attempt to transmit something like, "The other side is making a great deal of sense. I'd like you to modify your policy so that we can change our position." Your ratifiers (as they may begin to wonder where your loyalty really lies) respond with something such as, "We've heard all that before. Go back to the table and tell them NO, NO, NO!" So your team goes back to the table, and you tell the other team emphatically, "NO!" Now the other team cranks up some more data, more computer printouts, more experts, and some more "facts," and begins to sound even more convincing. So you return to your ratification hierarchy and say, "This is pretty good stuff. This is convincing material. You should really take a close look at it."

About that time, your ratifiers really begin to question your loyalty. They say to themselves, "Our negotiator is beginning to talk like the other side! Our person is going native! Whose side is this person on, anyway?" So you begin to negotiate with your own organization—on behalf of the other team. Think of it: you are actually working for the interests of the other side! Why? Because you, in some real sense, become the advocate of the other team with your own closer. Since the other team doesn't have a chance of getting direct access to your closers (if you have been effective in instructing your closer), the other team knows it must first go through you. If you and your closer have done your jobs well, your counterparts know they do not have a chance of getting what they want unless two conditions are met: (1) they must convince you of the reasonableness of their proposals, and (2) you must effectively represent their interest to your organizational hierarchy. In short, you must be able to sell their point of view back to your closers.

This works the other way around, too. *This is most important.* You want the other negotiator to become your advocate with his or her closers! This is the most important reason why it is so very critical to create and maintain a positive relationship with the other team. This is why you should not use tactics that surprise or destabilize the other team. This is why you must work to become reliable and trustworthy to the other team. The other team is the most attractive vehicle for your desired ends if you want a negotiated settlement. The other team (and/or your counterpart negotiator) is your instrument for getting what you want since he or she must be able to sell your point of view back to its closers. The two teams at the table, in an ideal negotiation, eventually depend on each other to represent each other's interests and to take care of satisfying each other's expectations!

Picture yourself representing the other party's position to your organization. If you have been as convincing as the other side has been, eventually your hierarchy will ask you, "OK, how much of a change in our policy do you want?" You might respond, "I recommend 100% change, so we can go back and perhaps split the difference. It will give us more bargaining room." Your closer responds, "How about a 10% change?" You respond, "How about 90% change?" And so on. Back and forth. You bargain with your own closer on behalf of the other team, and you should, if you are convinced to do so. Isn't that what you want the other party to do?

This bargaining with your organizational hierarchy happens as you try to move it off its bottom line. But too many times during a negotiation, this type of decision making is crisis driven—you run back to your ratifiers with a "hot potato," they frantically "jam around" and can't come to agreement and give it back to you. Then you go back to the table with their confusion to try to get an agreement.

Many times, your ratifiers may not even know, with certainty, what position they want to take, so your first job is to help them understand what they want to do. Why not be proactive rather than reactive? Why not convince your closers back home, when they first think of sending you to the table, to send you with clear instructions? You will be more confident and thus more convincing (and that sense will give you more personal leverage) and they'll get a better deal out of the other side. Why not begin to manage their expectations very early on?

Summary

In Part II, I have sketched a "core structural model" of negotiation. I've said that, contrary to the media's portrayal of a bilateral negotiation as a simple two-party affair, negotiation is in reality a multidimensional process that includes many basic structural dimensions: Figure (2) the horizontal negotiations with the other team, Figure (3) the internal negotiations within your own team, and Figure (5) the ratification negotiations between you and your organizational hierarchy and within your organizational hierarchy. I noted that successful, experienced negotiators have learned to manage the relationships along all the structural dimensions. Horizontal negotiation is characterized as taking place across the table and as an educational process where both sides have an opportunity to learn about theirs and the other side's real expectations. Internal negotiation is characterized as, among other things, the management of differences among the stabilizers (S) and destabilizers (DS) on a team by a chief negotiator who functions as a quasi-mediator (QM). Ratification negotiation is characterized as a negotiation with a team's closers, the people who sent it to the table.

In the next section, I'll begin to put it all together, and discuss in more detail how to effectively manage the structure, the information, expectations, time, behavior, your caucus, your hierarchy, your case(s) and the process of negotiation. In addition, the "best alternative to a negotiated agreement" (BATNA)* will be discussed and the importance of *not* destabilizing your counterparts so that you can better predict their behavior.

---

* BATNA: From Robert Fisher and William Ury's book *Getting to Yes.*

PART III

Putting It All Together: Managing the Structure and Process of Negotiation

In this section, we explore more in-depth how a negotiator can sequentially manage the complex multidimensional decision-making process found in most real-world negotiations. Most textbooks on negotiation suggest that the negotiation process may be divided into six sequential stages: planning, preparation, active meeting, the close, ratification, and implementation. I agree with this general division, but in this book we will explore how to manage the preparation; planning; active meeting; closing along the vertical, internal, and horizontal dimensions; ratification and implementation of the agreement. In addition, this part will deal with prenegotiating within each of the dimensions involved, working in the caucus, understanding "winners" and "losers," managing pressures, and the "scrimmage."

Managing the Ratification Dimension
Prenegotiating with the Organizational Hierarchy

While relationships along all of the three dimensions (ratification, internal, and horizontal) are important in all three stages of the negotiation process, probably the most important relationship to be managed during the planning and preparatory stages is the relationship with your organizational hierarchy. (See figure 6.)

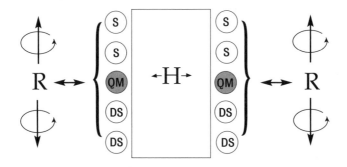

FIGURE 6

It is from your organization that you get your legitimacy, confidence, authority and power, and it is back to your organization that you must bring any final agreement for approval. If this phase of the negotiation has not been managed properly, it will be difficult, if not impossible, for you to effectively manage your team, the other team at the table, and the negotiation process per se!

Most of us have done it incorrectly for years. We allowed ourselves to be sent to the table with sketchy instructions at best, then we worked hard with the other team to hammer out common areas of possible agreement, and perhaps even fashioned a *tentative* agreement with the other side and attempted to "sell" our agreements to our organizational hierarchy. Because they gave us sketchy directions, they were surprised by the concreteness of the (albeit) tentative terms and often said, "No way." As a result, we lost credibility with our own organizational hierarchy and then we lost credibility with the other side, as well, in that we were forced to return to the table without approval of the tentative agreement. The subsequent table negotiations then became a form of "damage control," all of which could have been avoided if we had received clear instructions in the beginning.

Remember this old airline joke? The captain comes over the intercom and announces the good news and the bad news: "The good news is that we are making great time. The bad news is that we are lost." In a negotiation, if we don't know where we want to go—how long it will take us to get there, when to speed up, when to slow down, when to turn, when to stop—we'll never get there. And we won't know what to say when the person across the table asks us what we want or what we really expect. We'll end up sitting at the table and taking very protective, conservative and rigid positions, becoming defensive because of our insecurities since we don't know where we are going.

We may also be threatened by that negotiation, perceive all sorts of negative things going on, and interpret the other side's offers, information, smiles and goodwill as manipulations and attempts to deceive us. We may tend to be insecure about that particular negotiation and about the negotiation process as a whole. We may tend to bluff—the only alternative left us if we lack knowledge. Will the other team see our insecurity and insincerity? You bet! We will appear unprepared, insincere and incompetent, and it will cost us and eventually cost those whom we represent.

It may seem paradoxical, but the less freedom to close that you have at the negotiating table, the more confident and secure you will be concerning your team's situation during the negotiation. Your leverage as a negotiator at the table comes directly from the confidence you possess when you know where you are going—the ability to be believed by the other side because you know what you can deliver to your ratification hierarchy, your closer, your client, your boss. Who gives that power and confidence to you? Your organizational or ratification hierarchy, your client or your boss does. Thus, the most critical negotiations are the ones along the ratification dimension.

Your main job is to motivate your hierarchy to specifically define its position and, more important, its underlying interests and especially its expectations in the negotiation. Often, your own organization may not be very clear why it wants to get involved in a negotiation with the other side in the first place, so be proactive. Make it think about what it wants and expects out of the negotiation. Get its commitment. Demand that it be explicit about your limits.

At the same time that you are getting clear instructions and a clearly defined position, you must also prepare your organization to alter that position later. You must educate the people and manage their expectations about the likely reaction of the other side to their position—a position they are already having difficulty defining. You are, in effect, building a negotiation framework with your organization/client, and you are building some flexibility into that framework. This is not an easy job because of the way many organizations work, but a necessary one. Think of this phase as laying a solid foundation for a larger, complex building, perhaps a large mansion with many rooms.

There are differences within every organizational hierarchy. Just as no team is a monolith, no organization is a monolith—not in Western society. Relationships within organizations are complex. Most organizations are in some degree of disharmony. With respect to any particular issue, organizational differences likely manifest themselves the same way as individual differences do on a team. Individuals, and even whole departments, play the roles of the stabilizers, destabilizers, and quasi-mediators within the organization. Because of this organizational complexity, you must work to understand the complex correlation of forces determining your closers' positions, *i.e.*, the constraints that they are under. Understanding your organizational system means having good answers to questions such as: How do the closers make decisions? Who are the key players? Who wants the negotiation to succeed? Who wants the current organization's administration to fail? Who exercises power and how is it manifested? Who will be embarrassed by failure? By success?

What do you do with the knowledge of how your organization works? You manage it! Through your negotiating *and* mediating skills, harmonize the fragmented parts of your organization so that they work together and give you guidance that is as clear, explicit, and as comprehensive as possible. Don't hang back. For example, if you know someone would like to see the negotiation fail and to see your ship sink, what do you do? Approach the destabilizing people, section or individual, get their input, get them committed to a positive outcome, and tie them to the success of the negotiation. Fight the natural tendency to avoid interaction with the persons and/or entities you perceive to be against you, and try to avoid an end run. If you ignore those resisting your goals, you'll only be torpedoed later in the ratification process by those who have the power and inclination to do so.

When you spend time with your own organizational hierarchy prior to going to the table, you set the stage for your successful return. It may not be easy to interact with the organizational hierarchy at first, but your relationship with it could give you tremendous leverage within your team and with the other team. When you have negotiated well with your ratifiers, you can manage the rest of the negotiations more effectively; unfortunately, the opposite is also true. Remember the crucial importance of a firm foundation for a solid building. The information you gather relating to your side should be complemented by a concurrent gathering of similar information about the other side. More on this later.

Negotiating with Your Ratifiers Behind the Scenes While You Are at the Table: Keeping Them Informed

Just as important as getting good negotiating instructions and having a relatively short leash is keeping your organizational hierarchy informed of the progress of the talks. Keeping it informed gives you much more control over the process.

How much information should you share with the members of your organizational hierarchy? What should you tell them about the negotiations? A rule of thumb is to send them as much information as they can take. Then send some more until they yell, "Stop! We can't take any more information!"

Keeping them informed has a number of advantages. It helps them remain a part of the process and, since they have the final approval on whatever deal you make, that is very important. It also minimizes the likelihood that you will inadvertently surprise and destabilize them by giving them information which they have not been prepared to receive. It is especially important to keep the skeptics and destabilizers within your organizational hierarchy informed because they are the ones who are more apt to sabotage any agreement of which they are not a part. Finally, keeping them informed diffuses responsibility for the deal's implementation over the long haul.

As the negotiations proceed, your hierarchy's input will be woven into the fabric of the eventual agreement. Its members will thus be able to point to their contribution to the process. This allows minor adjustments throughout the process, and reduces the risk that they will balk at a final agreement because it is theirs.

Keeping them informed also protects you. They, in turn, will give you information that you need to process substantive decisions at the table. It will keep you informed about acceptable and unacceptable agreements and what the machinations back at headquarters portend for the negotiations. Keeping the ratification hierarchy informed prepares you for managing the troublesome departments or individuals to whom you may have to sell an agreement. Finally, this approach really *establishes the standards and criteria for success* and minimizes second guessing by others. In other words, using this approach assures your ability to keep *your* word! Checking to make sure your counterparts across the table have managed their hierarchy in the same manner will help assure that they will keep *their* word!

Closing the deal with your ratifiers. Near the end of a negotiation, when closure is approaching, the ratification hierarchy may want to get into the negotiation if you have created a good deal. Its entrance at such a late date can have a profoundly negative impact on a negotiation. The concern is that the entrance of your ratifier might be misread by your counterpart as having "more" to offer (unless that is part of your strategy). Therefore, one of the important prenegotiation negotiations with your organizational hierarchy is whether (and, if so, when) you should bring the chief executive officer (CEO) or some other heavyweight of the organization into the negotiation process. Since, (to paraphrase Confucius) "Success has a thousand parents and failure is an orphan," you may not have a choice.

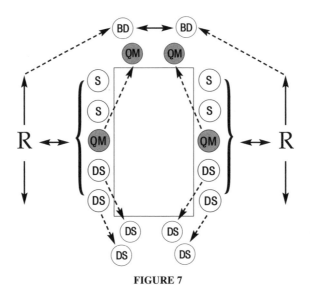

FIGURE 7

The "BD" in figure 7 stands for the "Big Dude"—your CEO. If the Big Dudes understand the negotiation process, they probably can't hurt you (though they probably won't help much, either). If they don't understand the process, however, they definitely can't help you; they can probably hurt you and the negotiations a great deal.

During prenegotiations, you can prevent that problem by managing your CEO. How? You tell your organizational hierarchy, "We may need the Big Dude in the negotiation." "Oh?" "Yes, but if BD comes in prematurely, it can cause problems since settlement is too far off to allow the Big Dude to look good." "Yes, we see." "But," you say, "if the Big Dude comes in too late, that may make it look like he doesn't have any real power. We'll tell you when it is appropriate to bring in the Big Dude without embarrassment of any kind."

What have you just done? With a little planning and a little prenegotiation with the ratification hierarchy, you have taken control of the process. You have gained control of the time when your CEO is to enter, as well as whether or not he or she should enter at all. This means that you can stage-manage the CEO's presence, including the time of appearance, duration, costumes, context, setting, depth of involvement and so on. And you have taken care of an important interest of the Big Dude, since Big Dudes do not wish to be embarrassed!

Occasionally, very early in a negotiation, even at the opening session, it may be advantageous to have your CEO appear at the table, as I noted earlier. If managed well, this can set the stage for the negotiation by showing the other side the importance of the negotiation to your side (or their side). But it is important to keep in mind that the CEO may be giving off hundreds of micro messages to the other side about what to expect out of the negotiation. This can be to your disadvantage unless these messages are managed properly.

If your CEO wants to appear in the middle of the negotiation to see what is going on, you should be even more cautious. Seldom is it wise to bring the "boss" into the middle of the negotiation process. Bosses have only a general idea of what has gone on. They are apt to send inadvertent messages that may lower the credibility of both your team and your organization. Be very careful that you understand the probable consequences of any such action. Additionally, the appearance of the Big Dude in the middle of the negotiation may destabilize the other side and jeopardize the whole negotiation because of the unpredictability of the behavior of both sides.

Occasionally, it may be desirable to bring the boss in at the end of a negotiation. This should probably be done very late, after all the work has been done, so that the appearance of the CEO is largely symbolic, a ceremonial gesture which I call "blessing the settlement."

The important point is that you should negotiate up front with your organization about the possible use of the CEO. If you are going to be held responsible for the success of the negotiations, it should be your decision when, and if, the BD enters the stage. The same caution holds with individuals at other levels of your organization who wish to come to the negotiation. If problems develop in this phase of the negotiation, you may decide to show this part of this book to those involved.

As I noted earlier, effectively managing the relationship with your organizational hierarchy may be the single most important thing you can do to ensure an eventual agreement. Managing your hierarchy includes prenegotiating the substantive and process issues with it, as well as keeping it informed of progress throughout the duration of the talks. If your ratification relationship has been well-managed, managing the internal relationships on your team will be easier. In the event that you and your boss disagree over a critical point, just keep in mind that, in this transaction, "ties don't count," and the word of the Big Dude is *the word*.

Managing the Internal Dimension

"Nobody said it would be easy
but they never explained how tough it would be."
—A.E. Berkeley

Prenegotiating the internal team dimension. One of the important things that happens during the preparation phase of a negotiation is the formation of the negotiation team. The way to begin managing your team is to have some input about its makeup and how it will work. You are seldom allowed to choose your team, but you will want a balanced mix of people. A good team includes individuals who are sufficiently similar to permit clear and effective communication. Your team needs to be able to speak the same language (figuratively as well as literally). On the other hand, you don't want a team of clones. So, it is also important to have a team which includes individuals who are different enough to permit a richness of perspectives. You may want to select a destabilizer you can manage. On the other hand, you won't want your team to become gridlocked and unable to proceed due to irresolvable social, cultural or ideological differences.

The content and context of any negotiation, of course, should be considered in determining the composition of a team. Clearly, knowledgeable people are an asset. The kind of talent you need depends on the subject of the negotiation. If the negotiation is about designing lunar landers, you will need someone with technical engineering expertise and experience in designing lunar landers. If the negotiation is about baseball contracts, you will need someone with technical and legal expertise and experience in negotiating or implementing baseball contracts.

Even so, technical and legal competency is not enough. In any negotiation analysis, if only the technological and legal aspects of the issues are considered, behavioral patterns may be overlooked. Some cultures, the Japanese for example, have a reputation for being very concerned with the process and with the behavioral aspects of relationships, including negotiations. Japanese companies routinely send their young managers to American business schools. The students are told to "just get to know Americans." They are not sent here necessarily for technical training. Can you imagine American companies routinely putting those kinds of resources behind "just getting to know" the culture and the people with whom they do business? One can hear the indignation now, "That would be like sending our young managers on a two-year vacation. And it would affect the bottom line. Let the foreign nationals learn to speak English!" So, the foreign nationals do learn English, and they learn how Americans think and behave. Then they know two languages and both sides of the relationship, while the Americans know only one. And people wonder why parts of the Japanese economy, such as the auto industry, have overtaken ours.

Many Japanese teams apply this behavioral emphasis to their negotiation strategy by designating individuals on their negotiating teams to be "process observers" whose responsibility is to observe the process of interaction, verbal and nonverbal behavior—in order to better understand the negotiation. They observe and listen for hidden messages on both teams, such as: Are the words of the spokesperson congruent with his or her nonverbal behavior? Who are the informal leaders? Who is confident? Who is trustworthy? Are they sincere? Are we perceived as sincere by them? How are we perceived by the other side? Is the relationship being strengthened or weakened by the behaviors observed? How might we better conduct the negotiations? Will the other side keep its word?

The important point to remember here is that, as Americans, we must not confuse technological expertise with process expertise. We must think through and address the process issues of a negotiation separately from the technological substantive issues. If we don't, the process aspect will inevitably be overlooked, and we will severely handicap the negotiation for both sides.

Both sides have a responsibility to understand just what is going on during the negotiation. This includes the responsibility for understanding our own and the other side's behavior, not simply the technical issues. Therefore, both technological and behavioral process expertise are necessary conditions for a successful outcome; neither alone is sufficient to guarantee the success of a negotiation.

While it is important to build a team that includes members with substantive, technical, legal, or behavioral expertise, you also want to include people who can take on a number of different tasks and thus play a diversity of roles. We often have a tendency to overload our chief negotiators. Negotiators will find that, at any given time, they will need to create strategy, set objectives, manage the information, take notes, draft agreements, and perform many other functions. There is no reason why these functions should be performed only by the chief negotiator. The skills, tasks, and responsibilities of a negotiator should be spread out among the negotiation team members. For more on the skills, responsibilities, and tasks of a negotiator, see Appendix E, on page 109.

Regardless of how a team is designed, however, you will likely end up with differences of opinion within your own team, and you will need to manage it. You will find it helpful for the negotiation if you can knit openness and discipline into the initial fabric of your team.

Openness. To establish openness requires leadership on your part and it will help to set the tone for an atmosphere of safety and trust. With an open group, you will be able to explore the talent and different perspectives of your group, and every member will feel like an important part of the team. In fact, the definition of a good team is a group of individuals who readily rely on each other, trust one another, and work well together to achieve common objectives and a common goal. This atmosphere insures creativity. The caucus session should feel like a "safe space" which allows free and candid expressions of opinion and emotion.

Discipline. A well-disciplined group is one that is ready to work as a team. When the time for discussion and debate is finished and a decision has to be made, a well-disciplined team will take responsibility for the leader's decision willingly, not grudgingly. The most effective discipline is not enforced by an authority from outside the individual, but is generated from within by each team member as a direct by-product of having clear goals and strategies, and having been involved in the setting of team objectives and tactics.

Organizing your horizontal negotiations. Once you have your marching orders and your negotiating team assignments fixed, a great deal of time must be spent researching the situation at hand. Ask yourself:

Who is on the other side?
How do they perceive the problem? The issues?
What are their expectations?
What are their touch points?
Do I have any personal contacts who are familiar with their organization?
What are their constraints?
What is their ratification hierarchy like?
How do they make decisions?
How stable is their organization?
Research the subject matter involved:
What are the issues in that area?
What's going on in the business world?

Now is the time to consider what experts you may need and to line them up.

Prior to the active meeting phase, establish signals and procedures for caucusing; lay out your respective positions; articulate your best alternatives; identify areas of mutual agreement and disagreement; identify the destabilizers and stabilizers on your team and theirs; anticipate what tactics they might attempt to use during negotiations; and assign someone to take minutes of the meeting. It is also very important to establish procedures for keeping the ratification hierarchy informed.

Prenegotiating team behavior for the active meeting phase. The most difficult dimension to be managed at the table may not be the horizontal dimension with the other team, but instead might be the internal dimension within your own team. Your team should understand how it will be managed during the negotiation before it sits down at the table.

Members need to know how the team will relate horizontally with the other side: Who will speak at the table; who will speak away from the table (off the record); whether notes will be sent or not sent and when notes will be passed. Well-trained teams, for example, would never send a note on the subject under discussion. Experienced teams would think through the implications of sending a note at that particular time in the negotiation process. Thus, team members have to think, "What nonverbal message are we sending by passing a note at this time? Is there a better time—a time when we will be giving a more innocuous signal?" It is especially important for members to know about caucus procedures. For instance, under what conditions will a caucus be called, who will call the caucus, and how will it be called? Let's look at Figure 8; it illustrates a team caucus.

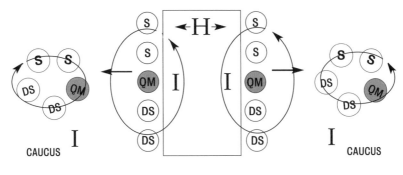

FIGURE 8

Caucus. The caucus is a team meeting. The arrow in Figure 8 points toward a small circle of S's, DS's and a QM. Amateurish teams conduct these internal negotiations in front of the other team or in public (at the table, in the hallway or at dinner), so the other team has absolutely no question as to who is agreeing and disagreeing with whom. More sophisticated teams caucus in private, out of sight, and out of earshot of the other team. They do this quite frequently. Effectively using the caucus is vital for you to negotiate successfully. If anything happens during a negotiation that you do not understand, that takes you by surprise, that makes you feel uncomfortable, rushed or off balance, call a caucus. You cannot caucus too much, but you can caucus too little.

A team should have its own understanding about when and how to call a caucus. The caucus is an important tool to help you manage the internal structure of your team, but it is also a tool to help you manage the horizontal structure of the other team. If you have not negotiated the process' ground rules, and the other side begins to act in a way that is unfamiliar to you or not in accordance with your perceptions of the ground rules, you will likely consider that to be in bad faith. If the other team acts as it is "supposed to act"—the way you expect it to act —trust is lessened. But if you have negotiated the process' ground rules, and you become confused at the table, you can take a break, talk it over with your own team, and then informally (and maybe off the record) ask for clarification from the other side, for its intentions, and so on. Recognize, however, that just as in passing notes and whispering to each other at the table, the context of when and how you call the break gives the other side information about your situation.

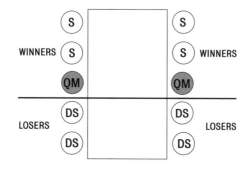

FIGURE 9

Closing the deal internally: winners and losers. As a necessary counter to the win/lose dynamic in the litigation model, where one side is judged the winner and one side the loser, interest has turned to portraying negotiation as a win/win opportunity. There is a great deal of reassuring talk in the popular press about how we all can get what we want from the process; how we all can increase the pie; how our side and their side can both win; and so on. This is not necessarily true. One is reminded of a carnival game where the big burly man with the booming voice exclaims, "Step right up! Step right up! Everyone's a winner!" Don't you bet on it!

First, the phrase win/win assumes several things: 1) that negotiation outcomes can be narrowed to two simple words (that the devil is not in the details); 2) that all of the negotiators on both sides of the table rate the outcome as a win; 3) that all of the involved hierarchies view the outcome as a win; 4) that the parties will really keep their respective promises during the implementation phase so that the win/win solution would be actualized; and 5) perhaps most importantly, that *all affected parties who were not represented at the negotiation table also view the outcome as a win.*

So you can see how the notion of win/win is not that simple when you really probe its meaning. It not only involves all the sides of the table, it also involves those who are not represented at the table, and those within each negotiating team.

The characterization of the negotiation process as win/win for both teams is also far too simplistic because during a successful negotiation, there generally are both losers as well as winners—somebody is usually bound to lose something. Who loses? It's likely that the destabilizers on both teams are the losers. But, there are winners on both sides of the table, too. To reach closure internally, at some point, you have to address the losers on your own team. Figure 9 shows the way the real win/lose pie is cut.

I have said that your role as a team chief is really that of a quasi-mediator—you mediate among stabilizers and destabilizers on your own team. At times during a negotiation, you might exchange your "mediator" hat for an "arbitrator" hat as you choose between the different views of your team members. This "arbitration"or decision making is frequently necessary as the negotiation process approaches closure and the destabilizers on your team attempt last-minute action to forestall or prevent agreement. If your team does not have norms of openness, this will be done without your awareness that there is still disagreement. The result will be that you (and the other team) may be "bushwhacked" by the destabilizers on your own side, and closure will be lost. That is why openness and discipline are important on your team.

Managing the Horizontal Dimension

Prenegotiation with the other side. The moment that someone in your organization telephones, writes a letter to, faxes, telexes, or even "bumps into" someone from another organization, causing a discussion to ensue about the possibility of a negotiation, the negotiation process has begun. The beginning of a negotiation is its most critical phase. The beginning may set the stage for all subsequent meetings. As mentioned earlier, mistakes can have lasting effects that color the final agreement or even prevent an agreement.

If someone in your organization has made a "botch" of something "small" such as sending an ambiguous e-mail (which is misinterpreted); sending a cold and formal initial form letter (which is perceived to be insulting); failing to return telephone call(s); placing a call which is perceived to be sarcastic, insincere or pushy or holding an awkward planning meeting (where the two sides make speeches at each other instead of planning together), the negotiation is already in trouble. You will probably find yourself digging out from under the effects of this type of incident from the moment you formally meet to negotiate with the other side until an agreement is finally fashioned, or both sides decide to call it quits.

Of course, there are some situations over which you don't have control in the initial contacts between your two organizations. Nevertheless, you can begin to have some control over the perceptions of both sides. You should, for example, think through the implications of what you do before you do it. You should take pains to query the other side regarding expectations about which you might have questions or concerns. You can also do your homework. As I said in Part II, learn something about the background of the proposed negotiation, as well as the important issues. Investigate the history of the relationship between your two organizations. Find out who on your side has had contact with the other party, and speak with that person. It also helps to know something about the people on the other team— who they are as individuals, as well as how they negotiate. You can put all this information to good use by conducting a "scrimmage."

Scrimmage. The "negotiation scrimmage" is a variation of law school case preparation. Law students are taught to never prepare just their case for trial. They are taught to prepare two cases—their own and the other side's. The same holds true for negotiation; you should be intimately familiar with both cases. Put yourself on the other side, and learn where it is coming from.

Divide your team, and have half of its members prepare and role play as the other side of the negotiation. Then scrimmage. If your team can sit at either side of the table and work both sides of the issues, imagine how well-prepared you will be for the real negotiation! If you think that scrimmaging is a waste of valuable time, you are missing the essence of preparation. Scrimmaging not only saves time, it positively affects the outcome of the negotiation. If your case is headed for adjudication, such as court, administrative law proceeding or arbitration, *and* there is a possibility that the case may be negotiated to settlement, then you might wish to prepare *four* cases—yours and theirs for adjudication and yours and theirs for a negotiated settlement.

After getting clear, explicit and comprehensive instructions from your organizational hierarchy, preparing and scrimmaging among your team members and managing the initial contacts with the other side, it is time to meet at the table.

Negotiating Horizontally at the Table

The pressure cooker. Sitting at the negotiation table has sometimes been compared to sitting in a pressure cooker. There are many kinds of pressures impinging on the negotiation teams: pressures from their organizational hierarchies, the internal differences on their own teams and, of course, pressure from across the table. The pressures are considerable, but they can be managed if they are known. The experienced negotiator has learned to manage information, as has been discussed earlier in this book. The experienced negotiator also learns to manage pressures by identifying the sources of the pressure and, when necessary, lessening those pressures on his or her own team when appropriate.

Here are some activities in which you can engage to reduce the pressure on your own team as you negotiate: (1) realize that you have control of the process; (2) avoid destabilizing the other team unnecessarily; (3) notify the other team of your intentions; (4) conduct the negotiations in private; (5) treat the other side with respect, (6) have a good BATNA; and (7) manage the time and information variables. These seven pressure reducers are discussed in order below.

1. You have control of the process. As you seat yourself at the negotiation table, it is important to remember the First Rule of Negotiation: There are no assumed rules. The negotiation process is a joint decision-making process. Both sides define the ground rules and parameters of the negotiation with each other. Nothing can be done unless you agree to it—explicitly or implicitly, by action or inaction. You both decide what information constitutes "fact" and what information does not constitute "fact." And you both decide when an agreement is acceptable enough to be recommended back to your respective organizations.

2. Avoid destabilizing the other team. We have continuously stressed the central importance of trust—in the sense of reliability, predictability, and credibility—as the cornerstone of the relationship between parties in a negotiation. In a typical opening move, an inexperienced negotiator might think it is advantageous to misrepresent his or her bottom line by as much as possible. This may be a serious mistake, because it may appear to others as insincerity when the misrepresenting negotiator eventually changes the position to one which is closer to the other side's initial proposal.

3. Notify the other side of your intentions. Avoiding destabilizing the other side also means that you should not surprise the other side. The inexperienced negotiator too often believes that, if one wants an advantage in the negotiation, one should surprise the other side. This is a mistake; surprise will destabilize and upset the other side's members. They will trust you less, which harms the relationship, but in addition, you will be disadvantaged by their unpredictable response. Their unpredictability is bad news for you because you should always try to move in such a way as to be able to predict the responses of the other side in order to manage the negotiation and steer it along. *To the extent that you can't predict its response, you have given up your management of the negotiation process.*

Thus, notifying your counterparts early about any irregularities has at least five advantages: (1) it gives the relationship stability; (2) it gives you credibility; (3) it increases the likelihood that they will trust you; (4) it gives you an advanced warning of their probable reaction (this is very useful information to have); and (5) it gives you time to change your mind before you get publicly or officially locked into a position which could prove to be embarrassing.

4. Conduct the negotiations in private. All of the real work in a negotiation is invisible to outside observers; probably 90% of significant undertakings occur beneath the surface. I believe that the reason we know so little about the negotiating process is that one of the central characteristics of

the process is its inherent privacy. The process contains within itself the principles of secrecy; without it, effective negotiation cannot occur. Why?

As we have learned, within the ratification, internal, and horizontal dimensions of a typical negotiation, stabilizers, destabilizers, and quasi-mediators interact in a complex web. Basic to the process of negotiation is the discussion of tentative and exploratory proposals. The exploratory nature of these kinds of interactions necessitates privacy. If they are leaked and made public, they typically become ammunition in the arsenals of one or another of the destabilizers. These destabilizers may not be actively involved in the actual negotiation. For these reasons, the "private" negotiation table is potentially a public platform, and the substantive issues, especially the difficult ones, are usually dealt with informally and in private between representatives of the different sides. No matter how private and secret negotiations at the table appear, experienced negotiators assume that the meeting at the table is a potential public event, and one day may be proven to be correct!

5. Treat the other side with respect. When two opposing trial lawyers "argue" a case in court, they often treat the other party, opposite counsel, and the other side's witnesses in a rough manner, while they treat the judge in the courtroom, administrative law judges at administrative hearings and arbitrators at arbitration hearings with deference and respect. Why? Because those deciders have the power to determine the facts, the outcome of the entire process, the remedy, and thus the fate of each party to the case.

Since we know that in a negotiation both sides are the deciders of fact and fate, you should treat the other side like you would treat a judge you are attempting to convince—with respect. Treat the other party as you would treat someone who has the power to determine whether you get what you want and expect. You don't know who on the other side just might turn out to be your advocate.

6. Have a good BATNA—Best Alternative To A Negotiated Agreement. One of the most important things that you can do to prepare for a negotiation is to have an alternative, or a pocket full of alternatives, before you even sit down at the table. This is the best way to reduce the pressure on your team.The better the alternative, the less pressure you feel. For instance, if you have six great job offers already, you won't feel much pressure during a seventh job interview. If you have commitments from three separate car dealers for a particular new car at dealer cost, you won't feel much pressure negotiating for the same model at a fourth dealership. This usually means, of course, that you must actually engage in alternative negotiations in order to develop acceptable alternatives.

7. Manage the time and information variables. Other things being equal, if one person in a negotiation is looking at his watch while another

person is looking at her calendar, the person looking at the watch is already at a disadvantage.

It is reported that, when the American delegation went to Paris in the early 1970s for peace talks with the North Vietnamese, the American representative, Averell Harriman, rented a room at the Ritz Hotel on a week-to-week basis. The North Vietnamese took a two-and-a-half-year lease on a villa outside of the city. I have heard different renditions of this story, but this one example provides a lot of information about what kind of time frame each side had, possibly about how serious each side took the negotiation, about what kind of a deal each side would get out of the ultimate agreement, and about which side probably felt more time pressure at the negotiation table.

Another example of time concern occurs when you take a flight to the coast to negotiate a deal with another organization. Do you have a return flight on your ticket? If you do, you are announcing to the other side when you will be leaving, and you are implying that you would like to nail down an agreement before you "must" leave. This puts you in an unnecessary time crunch, and, as you approach the deadline, you may tend to make concessions in order to reach an agreement. If the other side is sophisticated, it will know this and plan the negotiation in such a way as to elicit those concessions. So, when you travel to a negotiation that is important to you, you might consider arranging an open ticket and an open hotel reservation. In any case, do not necessarily inform the other side of your time constraints, even with regard to indirect matters such as the day and/or time of your flight. The humorous "Parkinson's Law" that states: "90 percent of the hard negotiation takes place in the last 10 percent of the time allowed for it" has a great deal of truth, and may be used against you. However, if it is to your advantage to force closure, I offer advice which is just the reverse.

Not all negotiations can be as open-ended as the Paris peace talks were for the North Vietnamese. Collective bargaining negotiations between labor and management often take place under a deadline imposed by the expiration of a contract and the threat of a strike. Like two opposing attorneys settling the lawsuit on the steps of the courthouse minutes before the trial is to begin, labor and management often use the deadline to move the collective bargaining process forward. They commit themselves to a course from which they have little recourse. In a sense, they are like poker players upping the ante, hoping that the other side runs out of time or money before they do and is forced to fold.

This is a similar time dynamic to the one we witnessed during prenegotiations with ratifiers (when one might desire a fairly clear and restrictive set of internal instructions), or when the auto salesperson checks back with the manager (and returns with a "no deal" response). In all of these situations, you are essentially committing yourself to an impersonal outside force over which you have no control. There is a very significant difference between the commitments you make in order to restrict yourself internally, and the commitments you make across the table to the other party during the course of the negotiation. The management of information, like the management of time, is situational. The one principle to appreciate is that no information is inadvertently given. Period! In a negotiation, information is transmitted in writing, verbally, and through the body language of the spokesperson and the team members. 'Nuff said.

Summary

In sum, this chapter took an in-depth look at the negotiations that must occur within each of the ratification, internal, and horizontal dimensions of the overall negotiation process. I placed an emphasis on the importance of the relationship with the organizational hierarchy—on motivating the hierarchy to specifically define its positions, interests, and expectations, on keeping them informed, on including the most resistant, and including the Big Dude, or CEO.

Internally, the negotiation team will also be negotiating amongst itself 1) in its formation—deciding on members and the roles they will play; 2) in deciding strategy; 3) during caucus; and 4) in closing a deal acceptable to each team member.

The horizontal negotiation is an act of managing multiple pressures. You can reduce the pressure on your team as you negotiate by 1) realizing that you have control of the process—nothing can be done unless you agree to it; 2) building trust by staying consistent and predictable—avoid surprises and destabilizing actions; 3) notifying the other team of your intentions—again, trust building; 4) conducting the negotiations in private; 5) treating the other side with respect; 6) having and knowing your BATNA; and 7) managing the time and information variables.

In the following section, I'll summarize the essence of the horizontal negotiation process. This pulls together many of the fundamental concepts and examines the heart of the process. In addition, this next section deals with the style of a negotiator as the negotiator works to be more convincing and persuasive by learning to be more "in touch" with the other party in terms of its interests and expectations for the sake of a good relationship. This section will also discuss some tips on note-taking, managing table information and shadow negotiations and ethics, as well as a full discussion on when and how to negotiate future dispute settlement systems in order to keep the relationship stable enough to afford an opportunity for parties to implement the remainder of their commitments.

PART IV

The Fundamentals of Table Behavior

Table Manners and Tips on Persuasion

"What would you do if I sang out of tune?
Would you stand up and walk out on me?"
—The Beatles, "A Little Help from My Friends."

The one-third concept of communication. In negotiation, communication takes place on three key levels: the words we select; the body language we use, including facial expression; and the tone of voice we use, including sounds we do or do not make. Most people fail to realize the importance of tone of voice and miss valuable clues to the other side's position. Be conscious of the way in which you and your team communicate, and look closely at the way the other side communicates.

The rolling ball concept of negotiation. Many negotiators are uncomfortable with silence and think in terms of the next concession in order to "keep the ball rolling." Learn to be comfortable with silence; overcome the impulse to fill the void. Silence is a valuable tool, particularly if the other side is uncomfortable with it. You can learn a lot just by watching the other side trying to hastily fill the void.

Exchanging information. I have said that the essence of negotiation is the exchange of commitments and promises. When negotiators trust one another, they open themselves up to having doubts created in their minds. This involves a process of mutual education in which there is an exchange of information, but for both sides to be effective, they must be able to persuade the other side. When I am negotiating with you, I want to know one thing above all else—how to convince you (not just of what to convince you, but how to convince you) to be my advocate when you recommend my settlement terms to your ratifiers. For tips on how to convince those that do not think the way you do, I encourage you to examine Appendix C (page 89), entitled "Styles of Persuasion."

How do you get information from your counterparts without causing them to show weakness, and how do you give information without showing weakness yourself? To gather information, demonstrate attentive behavior and listen. Gather all the information you can so that you can analyze it later and decide what is relevant and material. Look directly at the speaker during negotiations. Have someone who really understands the negotiation process take notes. It is difficult to be spokesperson and also take notes.

To give information without giving away your position, try not to make statements. Use sentences that begin: "If…, then…," or "If you could…, then I would try to…" Try not to say, "I will not do this or that" as an assertion. Rely on the more obscure "mealymouthed" words of a negotiator until intentions are clear.

Ask questions. The way experienced negotiators educate one another—the way they manage information, persuade, and create doubts—is not accomplished by making statements, but rather through asking questions. Asking the "right" question is the best way to find out what members of the other side want, what they expect, and even where they doubt their positions, and thus how to convince them. If it helps my case, I'll accept your assumption-based information as "fact." If it hurts my case, I'll question your assumptions and even the credibility of your fact-based statements. The point is to gather information by asking appropriate questions and listening attentively with empathy to everything the other side communicates (verbally and nonverbally), then choosing certain statements as targets for rebuttal or questioning. Asking open-ended questions, much like an informal direct examination, is preferable.

Take better notes than the other side. Negotiators can increase their authority with the other team by simply keeping an accurate record of what has happened and what has been said. The role of note takers in negotiations is a crucial one and is far more important than a mere clerical task. Taking notes of meetings and phone calls with the other side has many advantages: it gives you material for the difficult analytical work that your team does between meetings, as you search for proposals which encompass both sides' expectations and interests; it gives you a record for your organizational hierarchy; and it gives you more control over the memory or history of the table process. Go over your team's notes until everyone on your team agrees that they are accurate. Then, in the joint sessions, find an opportunity to compare your notes with the other side's—yours will be better! Soon, the other side will be relying on your notes.

Whoever controls the notes controls the memory of the negotiation. Whoever controls the memory controls the entire process.

Empathize. The ability to imagine oneself in another's situation, to appear to be at least interested in "walking in another's moccasins," and to identify with the feeling of another is an important attribute of successful negotiators. It is a skill that is developed over time with experience.

Paraphrase their statements. Rephrasing the other side's words in your own clear and simple terms will go a long way toward giving you control over the substantive aspects of a negotiation. One of your jobs as a negotiator is to interpret what the other side says. Getting the agreement of the other side on your paraphrasing allows you to control the language of the negotiation. If you do this often during the meeting, you will begin to define the shape of the settlement with specificity.

Backtracking. In his book, *In Search of Excellence*, Tom Peters coined the phrase "backtracking." This is a technique which allows the other person to reflect on his or her statement when you repeat it exactly as stated. Backtracking really affords an opportunity to repeat to the speaker his or her exact words—exactly as expressed in the exact tone, with the exact rate of speech and decibel level. Hearing his or her words from another party may give that original speaker pause...and the opportunity to amend or retract his/her words, tone, or intensity.

Summarize often. This will permit you to consolidate your control over the whole process. The summaries can be verbal at the meetings, but should be formally typed and agreed upon by the other side. You will probably find yourself negotiating with the other side over the wording of the summaries. Getting agreement on your summaries protects you from problems with the other side if it later tries to assert that you agreed to something you haven't, and thus keeps its members from wedging in any last-minute concessions from you.

Problem solving. Analyzing tactics used in negotiations while you are in the active meeting phase is like moving inward from the outer circle. Make sure you have a solid understanding of the professional ethics, organizational culture, and goals of the negotiation. Your response to a situation must be couched in terms of the other side's expectations, ethics, culture and goals, as well as your strategy, expectations, alternatives and objectives. Consider your expectations of the meeting and the power of implementation and enforcement of the prospective agreement. When presented with an unexpected maneuver, consider who, what, when, where and why the other side is using this tactic.

Ask more questions. Who initiated the tactic? Is it the other side's spokesperson or someone who is a destabilizer on the other team? What is that person's role on the team? What is your role on your team? Who else is in the room? As has been mentioned before, tactics are often meant to bolster a fellow team member rather than to destabilize you. Where the event takes place is also important. Can you walk out of the building if the other side has offended you? What are your alternatives?

An important clue for you to consider when weighing your response is exactly when the tactic is undertaken.Who gains if substantive negotiations are delayed while the tactic is being addressed? Tactics that are meant to appease members of the team posing them are usually undertaken early in the negotiation process. By the close of the negotiation, the discussions should be very straightforward if the parties intend to settle.

Why is the tactic being used? Is it just a bluff or an attempt to destabilize the team? Is it a legitimate tactic? Is it the result of cultural or socio-economic differences? No matter what the answers are to the above questions, take the time to consider them. Do not react emotionally to the situation. Buy time so you can analyze the situation and gain control again. Call for a caucus. Do it now.

Problem-solving emotional exchanges. Managing the negotiation also means managing your behavior and the behavior of the other team and your own team. The interactions across the table do not always go smoothly. Emotions are always lurking in the wings, waiting for an opportunity to be expressed. As a result, you may find yourself on the receiving end of an angry assault. Experienced negotiators frequently use the exchanges across the table to problem-solve; they do this by asking questions. If your counterparts make a speech insulting your side, use this to problem-solve. Ask yourself questions: Why are they doing this? Who is their audience? Is it really addressed to your team? Are they playing to the folks back home? Is it for the press? Are they having internal problems? Is the speech maker in a precarious position with members of his or her own team? Who is the speech maker? What kind of messages are the other members of the team communicating as the speaker harangues your side? Is the speaker trying to maximize the importance of a concession he or she is about to make or to embarrass you? Should you take it personally? Is the speaker trying to anger or intimidate you so that you break off the negotiations? What is going on? How do you control the situation?

Responding to Tactics

Some members of the other side may try to intimidate you through personal insults such as questioning your negotiation authority, losing their emotional control (whether real or feigned), remaining silent, isolating or ignoring you. They may also attempt power plays, such as using their personal influence and going directly to the top of your ratification hierarchy or walking out of the negotiation. They may attempt to manipulate you by playing good guy/bad guy routines, demanding one more "little" concession at the close or trying to "guilt trip" you.

Avoid emotional responses to any such tactics you perceive as intended to distract you from your goal/strategy/objectives/tactics. Buy time, if you need it, to cool off by remaining silent, asking your counterpart to repeat the statement, paraphrasing what was said or caucusing. Before you react, try to separate the people from the tactic and the message from the messenger.

Depending on your perception of the purpose of the tactic, you can choose to disregard the tactic and stay focused on the merits of the problem. You can also respond in kind to the other side: If its members are being uncooperative, be equally uncooperative. Another option is to identify the situation and address it directly. Humor is also an effective tool which can lighten a dark mood. Finally, you might openly question the legitimacy of the tactic. Query the other side whether its tactic furthers productive resolution of the dispute.

Take notes. Taking notes slowly and unobtrusively manages (controls) your counterparts' anger. Say, "Excuse me. I want to get this down. This is important." If you want to manage the members' boisterous behavior at the table, ask them to speak more slowly as you write down what they are saying. It's impossible for anyone to yell slowly!

Talk to the boisterous members in private, or talk privately to someone who can control the boisterous members. Experienced negotiators seldom want to make a move unless they can predict what the results of the move will be. For example, if they do not know why the other side is haranguing them, they will try to find out prior to deciding on an action. The way to find out is to ask the other side. Don't ask at the table—that may create a public embarrassment and backfire on you—ask alone and in private. You might say, "You were really yelling at us today. I felt insulted, and I'm having difficulty holding important members of my team at the table. Was that your intention? Is this the best way for us to discuss our mutual interests and expectations? Because if it is, perhaps my side should begin haranguing your side the same way tomorrow. What do you think?" Listen to the messages behind their responses. Then tell them what your side will do if they continue, and then do it to maintain your credibility and predictability.

Tell them. A "hard" negotiator might react to haranguing by members of the other side by becoming defensive, insulting them in return or by walking out—often without ever asking for an explanation, and without giving them the option to determine how the negotiations are to continue. A "soft" negotiator might fear that playing tit-for-tat, putting them on notice that "our side will unleash 'Conan' if you continue to harangue us with 'Rambo'" will jeopardize the relationship and the negotiations altogether. "Experienced" negotiators know that notifying the other side of your contingent intentions, and then acting in accordance with your notification when the contingency arises, will actually strengthen the relationship because by acting consistently, and thus predictably, you gain credibility.

"Tell it like it is."
—Aaron Neville

Managing the Closing of the Deal Across the Table

At some point in the negotiation, the other side may probe to find out about the relationship between you, your team, and the hierarchy or client that you represent. This can be either a legitimate search for information, and/or a tactic to throw you off balance—a destabilization tactic. As a legitimate search for information, the question can approximate:

"Who are the closers on your side?"
"Are they at the table?"
"Where are they in terms of a status in the hierarchy?" and
"How do I convince you to convince them that our case has merit?"

As a tactic to destabilize your side, the questioners might ask, "Do you have the authority to negotiate?" Do you? Of course you do! Tell them that! "Yes, I have the authority to negotiate; my authority comes from my organizational hierarchy/client/ratifiers/whoever." A more sophisticated probe or destabilization tactic on the part of the other side is: "Do you have the authority to consummate an agreement? Do you have the power to close?" This is clearly intended to shake your confidence and self-assurance. An effective response to that question is, "I have as much authority to close as you do." And you are probably right.

Again, before you get hooked by such questions, keep in mind that you may not really want to have the authority to close (or you may not want the other side to perceive you as having the authority to close if you, in fact, have it). Remember the advantages gained by the car salesman who had to check with his manager—after you had made what you had thought was a reasonable offer. The car salesman only promises to recommend while the customer promises to act! Authority to effectively recommend is more powerful than the authority to close without recourse to a ratifier in most situations.

How do you know if you are approaching closure? As the negotiations progress, and both sides may become more comfortable with each other, you will begin to see changes in the tenor of the negotiations. The person on the other side of the table—your opposite number—may be struggling with the same issues that you are. As you begin to work more closely with your opposite number to discuss the negotiation, which you should, you will both begin to discover you have the same job and similar problems.

So how do you know when you are approaching closure? When you are openly sharing expectations and when you are talking freely and relying on each other to take care of the problems on each other's team and/or with each other's hierarchy/client. Two problems are paramount: making the critical recommendation and managing the destabilizers.

Close on "your" words. If, as we discussed earlier, you have paraphrased your counterparts' words into your own; taken good notes; and made good summaries of the discussions, you have helped to put your side in a position to "close" the agreement in your own words. If you have ensured agreement on the small points covered along the way, whether they seemed important or not, you have done a lot to define the final written agreement. In every negotiation there are "two" negotiations: the verbal negotiations and the negotiations over what words to choose to accurately reflect the intentions of the parties. The written words are what count to a judge, arbitrator or implementer of the deal.

The recommendation and ratification. For a negotiation to succeed, both sides will have to go back to their respective organizational hierarchies at some time and recommend the other side's point of view to some degree. If the table negotiations have been successful up to this point, the currency of the negotiation then becomes a commitment or promise by each side to recommend to its respective ratifiers a joint proposal that will appear to be a "sell out" to an uninformed hierarchy. Thus, both negotiating teams may be simultaneously suspect in both houses. Team discipline is imperative here—both teams need to have their destabilizers on the side of the prospective agreement.

The destabilizers. A private meeting between team chiefs also gives you the opportunity to swap information on how the two of you will have to help manage the problems of each other's teams. You might say, "I've got pain dealing with my team," meaning you are having trouble with the destabilizers on your team. The other team chief might say, "You think you have pain, I've got real pain; you should be managing my team." Some chief negotiators, if trust is strong between them, may begin to rely on each other. For example, you may find it necessary to rely on the other team's chief to manage your destabilizers, and he or she will then have to rely on you to explain how. You know your team members better than the other side does. You know where your own destabilizers have doubts. You can help your opposite number take care of your destabilizers when you reveal information about the kinds of things that would help you persuade your own destabilizers. Likewise, the other side's chief may have to rely on you. These problems are frequently handled in private, off-the-record or "shadow" negotiations between the two chief negotiators or "quasi-mediators." It is important to note that serious ethical questions arise when this occurs. It is also important that any book on negotiation deal with this phenomenon to some extent.

Shadow Negotiations

What are some of the advantages and disadvantages of a one-on-one summit between the two chief negotiators (QM to QM)? Let's look at Figure 7 again.

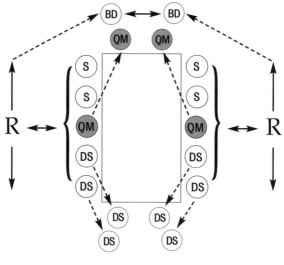

FIGURE 7

The principal advantage is that it affords negotiators the privacy to take risks and to be more creative. I can make you an offer, a tentative proposal, and present it to you in private as an "if/then" syllogism: "If I were to offer you X, would you be willing to do Y? If you don't accept this offer, I'm going to deny that I ever made you the offer." (This is, I think, quite ethical, because you have the opportunity to respond this way: "If you're going to make me an offer with a denial attached, then I don't even want to hear it." It is not ethical for me to make you an offer, which you reject, and then subsequently deny that I ever made it. In the first case the denial condition is made in advance as part of the offer; in the second case, it is probably perceived as punishing and duplicitous and may be somewhat destabilizing.) You may need to exclude your team destabilizers and stabilizers from the private meetings—this is an off-the-record "walk in the woods" solely between the two chief negotiators.

There are also some disadvantages to private meetings between team chiefs. It can exacerbate suspicion on your team and make your internal negotiations more difficult, unless you have established the procedure of reporting back the important things that you discussed. It is generally unwise to have these one-on-one talks when you are configured as a team, *i.e.*, don't leave the table to have a horizontal caucus with your opposite number. Why not? Because the two teams will have the chance to interact with each other, and in your absence, they destabilize. If the stabilizers get together, they may raise the expectations of the other side. If the destabilizers get together, they may have enough power and enough muscle to tip over the whole deal. Unless you have a very good reason to the contrary, it is much wiser to limit the private exchanges to the team spokespersons and then to the whole team at informal gatherings and to let your team know that you will return with only a recommendation at best and not a "done" deal. This puts your team in the position of taking the responsibility for the "team" decision. Check to see if your counterpart has a similar decision-making procedure.

The stabilizers are easy to work with—for both their own team and the other team—but this isn't necessarily an advantage because stabilizers seldom have as much persuasive power within their own team or with their hierarchy as the destabilizers. Destabilizers, on the other hand, are more difficult for their own team and the other team to work with, but this isn't necessarily a disadvantage because if they can be convinced of the reasonableness of the other side's position, they often have the power and credibility to convince their own team and organizational hierarchy. For example, an arms-control negotiator who is a "hawk" will have an easier time selling an arms-control treaty to skeptics in his organization than a "dove" will. When you are at the table, you want the toughest person on the other team to be convinced, because when this person is convinced, he or she can sell the deal to his or her own team and ratifiers. We expect a "dove" to favor any agreement advancing the cause of peace; when a "hawk" supports such an agreement we listen very closely.

Implementation. A negotiated agreement is only a verbal commitment or promise written on a piece of paper unless, and until, it is implemented. The best—and in the final analysis, the only real—guarantee of good faith implementation depends on the trust and confidence that exists between the parties to a negotiation. The best way to ensure total compliance is to maintain a good relationship.

Again, it is important to keep in mind who the potential losers are in a negotiation—the destabilizers. Be aware of this as you proceed with negotiations, as well as when it comes time for implementation of the agreement. Destabilizers, like the phoenix, may arise from the ashes to torch a deal well after both sides have signed the agreement, shaken hands, and walked away from the table thinking that a fair agreement had been made. You may thus have to manage the ratification and implementation process within your own organizational hierarchy. This can take much work. It is the final step in the formal negotiation process and may take more time and attention than the table negotiations.

One final suggestion: In an ongoing relationship, the best way to begin your next negotiation is to already have a good working relationship with the party from your previous negotiation. In this sense, you should strive to make the negotiation process continuous, an integral part of the "business as usual" relationship, and not an isolated event.

Enforcement. Exchanging promises and commitments is only the first step in formulating a positive working relationship. The second important step is the keeping and enforcement of promises—the promise-checking phase of negotiation. At the negotiating table, especially during the eleventh hour, there may be a rush to agreement in principle with no serious discussion of language or implementation of the terms of a deal. Indeed, sometimes the agreed language is intentionally kept vague by both sides so that it can be acceptable to each party's ratification hierarchy.

The problem then comes later, once the two parties are living day-to-day with the contract, when disagreements as to application and/or interpretation surface, as they inevitably will. The crucial point to remember is that problems of interpretation are inevitable—as long as there is more than one point of view, disagreements can't help but surface. It is necessary to provide *in advance* for mechanisms by which those disputes can be resolved peacefully, equitably, and with finality. The best time to negotiate a "future dispute resolution clause" is during the period of euphoria at the time of agreement and before any disputes arise. The worst time to attempt to create a dispute resolution system is when a serious dispute has already arisen, because at that time the parties are most angry at each other and mistrustful of each other's dispute resolution process suggestions.

What kind of dispute resolution system is best? There is no single answer; it depends upon the needs of the parties. Just as the first rule of negotiation is that there are no preset immutable rules, so too in the design of a future dispute resolution clause or system there is no one best system. Nonetheless, there are some basic concepts which are generally applicable when designing a more nonjudicial alternative to litigation.

Primarily, the parties ought to consider creating a system which provides for multiple opportunities to meet and voluntarily negotiate a settlement. If there is no negotiated settlement, with or without mediation, then an efficient means to provide a final and binding resolution is needed.

Perhaps one of the best examples of such a well-conceived procedure can be found in the area of labor/management grievance arbitration procedures. If any process has worked exceptionally well in the labor/management arena it is the negotiated grievance arbitration procedure. Some 95 percent of labor/management agreements contain such elaborate systems. Typically, when negotiating a first contract at the bargaining table, the parties jointly create a grievance or problem-solving procedure which covers disputes that arise over the life of the agreement regarding problems involving the interpretation and/or application of the language in the agreement as related to the "rights" of the parties.

Grievance procedures usually provide for multiple opportunities for the parties to meet and negotiate a mutually satisfactory settlement. Generally, these procedures are divided into phases which bring increasing authority applied to the case. These phases are designated as negotiating "steps" and provide for established time limits which need to be followed. For example, the first step of the grievance procedure may designate the grievant and union steward to meet with the line supervisor with authority to take the action in question. Most grievances are resolved through negotiation at this step by the person most directly involved in the problem. It is usually this person who has the most knowledge of the relevant information and the greatest personal stake in its outcome in a disciplinary matter.

If unresolved, the grievance moves to the second step within a prescribed time period, usually 10 workdays. At this step, members of each party's hierarchy with greater authority are involved and presume an increase in objectivity. For the employer, it may be an industrial relations specialist who meets with the chair of the local union's grievance committee. These two individuals often have an ongoing working relationship built over time, can more candidly discuss the grievances, and work to resolve through negotiation a large proportion of the grievances that reach their level.

Once again, unresolved grievances/problems will be moved to a third step, usually within a slightly longer time period of perhaps 14 workdays. At this level, the employer's industrial relations manager may meet with a full-time union representative. Here we have two highly professional employee relations specialists who can bring increased objectivity and experience in negotiation and problem-solving to resolve the grievance. The vast majority of grievances which reach this step are negotiated to settlement, and very few go to the final step, which is binding grievance (or "rights") arbitration.

It is important to note that even if a grievance is unresolved at the third step conference and the representatives prepare to go to arbitration, the negotiation process is by no means ended. As the representatives meet or speak on the phone to go about the tasks of selecting an arbitrator and making arrangements for the arbitration hearing, they may well seek to continue to resolve the grievance or problem. It is not uncommon to have the parties reach a settlement the morning of a scheduled hearing—or, because the arbitration hearing itself acts as a "discovery" process, even during a recess in the middle of a hearing or after the hearing. In addition, even if the case goes to an arbitration hearing, parties may negotiate many stipulations as to "fact" which save time in the preparation and presentation and help to insure a higher quality case heard by the arbitrator and thus enhance the opportunity for a more relevant decision, award, and remedy.

The key point here is that the grievance procedure belongs to the parties, and it is they who design and conduct it. They may create a fourth or even a fifth prearbitration step—perhaps employing the mediation process, if they jointly choose, or expanding time limits or even suspending them, whatever they both believe will work best. The process may change over time as they gain experience and learn what works and what doesn't. Recently, more and more parties have been adding a mediation step and/or a fact-finding step or a med/arb step (a combination of mediation with arbitration) to enhance efficient closure of grievances and problems. The mere existence of an arbitration clause enhances the viability of the negotiation and mediation processes.

Increasingly in many other sectors, such as insurance and construction, parties are taking the proactive approach that unions and employers have long pursued. They are discovering that it is best to plan how to resolve disputes before they arise, not after. Further, having a well-designed future dispute resolution system in place encourages faster settlements and engenders less bitterness all around. This is a definite paradigm shift!

Mediation/arbitration clauses. Med/arb has grown in popularity, especially during the past decade. Often the same well-respected neutral is selected to serve in both roles. Mediation, discussed more fully in the next part of this book, is the voluntary reaching of a settlement with the assistance of a third-party neutral. The mediation phase is often successful at resolving all outstanding issues, or at least in narrowing the gap between the parties' respective positions. In part, this high rate of success may be due to the skill of the mediator and/or the desire of the parties to fashion a settlement that better meets their needs and expectations instead of having one imposed by arbitral fiat. The controlling factor is the power the neutral has in med/arb. While the mediator's suggestions are not binding on either side, when the same individual who makes suggestions is at once going to be deciding the outcome as the arbitrator, one listens very closely to any suggestions, much like a settlement judge in a court of law. Indeed, the reason med/arb is so successful is that the "med" part of the process is backed by the "arb" part. Finally, there is an element of self-selection and voluntarism in that, first, the parties must jointly decide to engage in med/arb and, second, select a neutral in whom they repose great confidence. One wonders whether without the "hammer" of arbitration the mediator would be quite so successful at achieving resolution of the dispute in the med/arb process.

One also wonders whether the success of pure grievance mediation is due to the existence of the grievance arbitration clause for the very same reason. In Part V, which follows, I'll discuss with more detail many of the future dispute settlement clauses from which parties may voluntarily select.

Negotiation and Dispute Resolution

For many years we have been hearing about the increase in litigation, delays in the courts, and the need for more judges. As individuals and institutions have grown dissatisfied and frustrated with the traditional adjudication system, they have turned to alternative means of dispute resolution. Fifteen years ago, a grassroots effort was initiated to help citizens resolve their legal problems without the expense and delays involved in traditional court proceedings. These means of dispute resolution have allowed people to resolve their problems quickly, inexpensively and often more effectively because there are many kinds of disputes that do not benefit from adjudication.

It has been said that conflict is a growth industry. Forms of alternative dispute resolution such as mediation and arbitration are becoming increasingly popular. But "negotiation" is rather loosely subsumed under the rubric of "alternative dispute resolution" as one of the many such alternatives. To be sure, negotiation is frequently employed in the early stages of a dispute, but the process of negotiation is both broader and more fundamental than other methods of dispute resolution.

The array of dispute resolution processes falls along a continuum. At one end, the parties have complete control of the resolution of their problem, like negotiation. At the other end are processes that closely resemble adjudication, like arbitration, which render the parties very little direct control over the outcome but a great deal of control over the design of the arbitral process. In this part of the book I will describe the different dispute resolution processes that fall along that continuum and their relationship to negotiation. I will also explain some common terms of the negotiation process.

A. *Conciliation*. Often in the negotiating process the parties reach an impasse. Sometimes they need a third-party helper, such as a conciliator, to break that impasse. The third-party conciliator's work is to get the parties to literally sit across the table from one another but not to take part in their procedural and substantive decision making. Joint meeting space, caucus rooms, coffee, snacks, word processing help, telephones, and fax machines are commonly provided by the conciliator.

B. *An ombudsperson* is a third party who investigates and expedites complaints with the goal of settling the complaint or proposing more responsive changes in the system. The ombudsperson uses negotiation and mediation techniques. This model works best when the ombudsperson reports directly to the top operating officer in the institute. A number of cities and other governmental entities, as well as corporations, employ ombudspersons to resolve disputes about city service or employee complaints. An ombudsperson is often thought of as a fact finder. He or she acts as an independent evaluator who does not possess the authority to issue any final or binding decisions concerning the dispute. Parties have an opportunity to present their points of view to the ombudsperson who may then conduct an investigation of the situation. After considering all the "facts," the ombudsperson provides written advice as to what the parties should do, but, of course, they are not obligated to follow that advice.

C. *Mediators* are usually considered neutral third parties and engage in the same activities as conciliators, but they stay with the parties throughout the negotiations and make procedural decisions (with permission) but not decisions regarding the substantive issues. Mediators assist in communicating information regarding issues of a dispute between the parties and aid them in reaching an agreement. Mediators are very careful that they appear as neutral as possible, lest they make a negative impact on their acceptability and effectiveness. Once the mediator has gained a neutral posture, the parties, if they want a settlement, can use the mediator as a communication bridge to transmit information back and forth. A mediator fills a trust vacuum and works to serve as a reliable channel of communication. In international disputes the word "conciliator" is used as a substitute for the title of mediator as described here.

D. *Facilitation* is a useful process when negotiating the settlement of multiparty disputes. For example, the Environmental Protection Agency (EPA) may name as many as 140 Potentially Responsible Parties (PRPs) for dumping in a toxic waste area. That means individual PRPs have the EPA, the Department of Environment of that particular state, the Department of Justice, and the lawyers for 139 other PRPs to contend with in trying to resolve this situation. How do you manage this problem? In this situation, facilitation is helpful because facilitators can approach the actual responsible parties to determine how to apportion the percentages as to what each

company should pay in damages and clean-up costs. Facilitators use negotiation and mediation techniques to structure the case for the parties
involved. In the summary and conclusion portion of this book which immediately follows I have thought to include some additional insights regarding the multilateral model of negotiation which usually benefits from some
form of active facilitation because of the obvious complexity of this model.

E. *A fact finder* drafts out recommendations for a settlement by holding a somewhat formal joint hearing and accepts information as offered by
the parties. The fact finder may also divide the parties into two groups,
sketch out a draft recommendation for resolving the dispute, and work to
elicit each party's positive reaction to it. Lacking the power to bind the parties, the experienced fact finder keeps reshaping the agreement to meet the
concerns of the two sides until an agreement is reached. In the end, the fact
finder has taken care of both the verbal activity in the negotiations and also
the written agreement to which it tended. This is an effective process
because the parties are not threatened by it, and they themselves create a
product with the active substantive assistance of a neutral.

F. *Mediation/Fact-Finding.* The med/fact finder is expected to render
an advisory fact-finding report but actively uses mediation skills to get the
parties to "buy in" to the report prior to its issuance.

G. *Minitrials* are private, consensual proceedings where the presence
of the principal (client), the lawyer, and the insurance representative is
required in certain cases. A negotiated resolution is sought following an
expedited summary presentation of the best case for each party in a dispute with a neutral chairperson acting to manage the hearing. Following
the attorney's presentation and assuming some doubts have been created
in the minds' of both sides, the principals are expected to reassess their risk
factors and are often motivated to attempt to negotiate their differences
with the chairperson acting as mediator.

H. *Interest Arbitration.* The interest arbitrator is someone who, in most
instances in the absence of a contract or written agreement, will listen to
the parties at a formal hearing and eventually dictate the terms of an agreement. The parties are bound by his or her award either by law, such as the
protective services (police and fire) in the public sector, or by voluntary
mutual agreement, such as occurs in professional sports.

I. *Rights Arbitration.* The rights arbitrator has final and binding
authority over the application and interpretation of an existing contract.
Having been jointly empowered voluntarily by the parties, the arbitrator
determines the rights of the parties under the contract at issue, following a
demand to arbitrate by one or both of the parties to the contract.

J. *Mediation/arbitration* occurs when a third-party neutral has the
authority to make a decision but also possesses mediation skills. When
parties choose this route, they are essentially saying, "Look, we have

agreed to bring you in as a mediator/arbitrator. We feel comfortable that you will be fair and just in how you decide this case if required. However, we think that some of the issues will yield to mediation and we would like you to attempt to work with us to mediate them. The rest you will have to decide as an arbitrator."

K. *Med/Arb/Med*. Though the classic model is mediation/arbitration, med/arb/med is a flexible process that is also used. Here is an example of how this process is used: The case is initially mediated, but when impasses arise, the arbitration hearing begins as per a mutually agreed upon schedule. The parties can voluntarily pull back from the arbitration at any time, however, and decide to start negotiating again. The arbitration hearing itself thus acts as a discovery process and affords the parties an opportunity to reassess their chances in arbitration. The arbitrator then resumes the role of mediator.

L. *Arb/med* was described to me by Charles Nupen, director of the Independent Mediation Service of South Africa. Nupen explained that following his arbitration hearing, he reconstitutes the principal parties to the hearing after he has decided the case and sealed his opinion and award in two envelopes. Because the hearing acts as a discovery process, he offers the parties an opportunity to negotiate their differences at this meeting with him acting as mediator. Nupen explained that about half of his cases settle with the parties negotiating their differences, and Nupen, acting as mediator, never having to render his decision and award.

M. When parties use *private judges*, they hire a retired judge to arbitrate, mediate or serve as a fact finder in their dispute, according to their mutual agreement for empowerment of the neutral third party. The "judge" in many cases renders an opinion of how he or she would decide the case. In the analysis rendered by the judge, he or she discusses the most compelling "facts." This advisory opinion motivates the disputing parties to settle, as they now have an objective opinion of the worth of their cases.

N. *Litigation*, as we described earlier in the book, is the predominant form of dispute resolution in the U.S. It is costly and time-consuming, and the parties have little or no control over the process or the outcome. In this evidentiary process each party offers a theory on how substantive issues are treated in their respective cases; attempts to support their theory with their perception of the "facts;" offers evidence as proof of facts they allege to be true (under strict rules of evidence and proof); and presents arguments based on the preceding information. The judge acts as finder of fact and decides who wins and the appropriate remedy.

O. *Elective Process*. Elections are win/lose oriented and are designed to bring about closure or surface a decision through referendum. Although much negotiation takes place in the design of the election process itself, the actual decision is left to the electorate.

Summary and Conclusion

In this book, you have reviewed the process and structure of typical bilateral negotiations. I explained that the two-party structure reveals a multidimensional structure with negotiations along ratification, internal and horizontal dimensions. Many negotiations, however, are even more complex than bilateral ones. These complex talks are called multilateral negotiations and include the typical negotiations that take place at the United Nations, in environmental disputes, in inter-agency policymaking in the federal government, and in the planning of a town's Fourth of July celebration, etc. Figure 10 is an example of a multilateral negotiation.

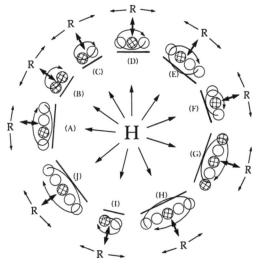

FIGURE 10

Managing the multilateral negotiation is, of course, much more complicated than managing the bilateral negotiation, principally because coalition formations become more intricate. Coalitions formed for one issue can readily dissolve for another, thus affecting trust relationships. The basic structural patterns of interaction and processes, though, are the same in multilateral settings as those we have sketched for bilateral negotiations. If you are aware of those patterns and understand them, you have a better chance of successfully managing any complex negotiation.

Figure 11 illustrates the increasing complexity of decision making when a bureaucracy is involved. Decision making in a multilateral negotiation must move within and from the ratifiers to the table negotiators and back to and through the various ratification levels. By understanding this model one can comprehend why, in the face of a natural disaster, it takes an inordinate amount of time for the federal government to provide relief to a local area even when the need is desperate.

This multilateral model can also explain the difficulties faced in government-to-government-to-government negotiations such as those occurring at the United Nations. When different cultural norms, different languages, and confusing communication through interpreters (who may or may not understand the negotiation process) are added to a negotiation, one can understand why many global problems are left unresolved. It may not be due to a lack of will within the parties, but because of the problems inherent in the multilateral negotiation model.

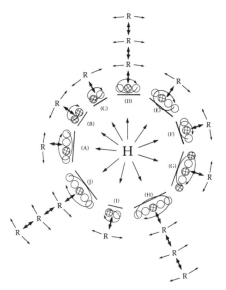

FIGURE 11

Finally, I have discussed the relationship of negotiation to the growing field of dispute resolution. Negotiation anchors one end of the dispute resolution continuum. It represents the process over which parties to a dispute have the most control, in terms of both the process and the ultimate outcome of the dispute. But negotiation is broader, since it is a fundamental component of the other forms of dispute resolution.

Before I summarize the ideas I have presented in this book, however, let me leave you with the lyric of an old song that captures the thought: "It ain't what you do, it's the way that you do it." That is to say, no list of insights or "rules" is an adequate guide for successfully managing a negotiation by itself. Any application of these insights requires good judgment on how and when to employ them. That is where experience is invaluable. In any case, here are the main points I covered in this book. See also my "Ten Commandments of Negotiation" in Appendix F.

Review:

—The essence of negotiation is a process that provides an opportunity through which the parties or disputants may exchange commitments and promises through which they resolve their problems and reach agreement.

—The relationship between the parties is the most critical variable in determining the climate and the ultimate outcome of a negotiation.

—Trust is the central issue of a relationship. Parties in a negotiation will not take the risks of having their minds and behavior changed without some degree of trust.

—The basic job of a negotiator is to create doubts in the other party as to the viability of its positions. Listen to what your counterparts try to communicate. Learn their expectations, positions, interests, problems, perspectives, assumptions, and values. Then create doubts in their minds about the viability of the first six.

—Many misperceive negotiation and confuse it with an adversarial process, such as adjudication in a courtroom, but it isn't. Negotiation is a joint decision-making process where the parties have the power to determine the "facts" and decide the outcome, instead of a third-party decider of fact and fate.

—The first rule of negotiation is that there are no rules for your particular negotiation, unless you first negotiate them with the other side(s).

—Real power in a negotiation is the ability to be believed.

—Manage your counterparts' expectations. For example, begin to lower their expectations early in the negotiation. Later, however, should they begin to lose hope that an agreement can be reached, you may need to raise their expectations to convince them that an agreement is possible.

—Time is a critical variable to be managed in a negotiation. If you are looking at your watch and another person is looking at the calendar, you're already in trouble. Patience is more than a virtue—it is a necessity.

—Managing your own behavior is critical, as it provides a role model for members of your team and the other team. People emulate leaders.

—Do not wait until the actual "contact hours" to manage resources. This should be completed prior to informal or formal contact time.

—Manage information. The main reason to have only one spokesperson on your team is to assure the information your team designed to be conveyed to the other side has only one source. In addition, your team members should be trained to minimize confusion by managing their body language.

—Describing negotiation as a "win/win" scenario oversimplifies the process. The real winners are those on both sides who benefit from the negotiated agreement. There are losers—they are the ones who perceive that an agreement has worked or will work against their interests. They are usually the destabilizers.

Ratifiers

—Negotiations have a multidimensional structure comprising: (a) the ratification relationship of one's negotiating team with one's organizational ratifiers: (b) the internal relationships among quasi-mediator, stabilizers, and destabilizers; and (c) the horizontal relationship across the table with the other side.

—Get clear instructions from your organizational ratifiers. This gives you confidence in where you are going, and the increased confidence will increase your effectiveness because you will be more convincing.

—Keep your organization informed during the talks and be aware of the internal negotiation that is always going on within your organization's ratification hierarchy.

—Authority to negotiate is given to you by your organizational hierarchy. You should not want more than the authority to negotiate.

—Authority to "close" usually remains with the organizational hierarchy, which is where it belongs since you will ask for concessions from the other side in order to "sell" your ratifiers.

Internal

—Prepare both cases for a negotiated settlement with your team before you go to the table; if the case might be litigated in arbitration or in court, you must prepare all four cases.

—Address process and substantive issues separately. Have your process observer at the table with you.

—Assign roles and responsibilities to your team members such as process observer, time keeper, note taker, technician, legal advisor, etc.

—Create a team norm of openness and discipline, and agree on a system of how your team will make decisions.

—Caucus often, but in private.

—Debrief with your team after each session, and periodically work with your team to perfect your notes. Once made perfect, test the notes in front of the other team so they will begin to rely on your team's notes.

Horizontal

—Always use correct social courtesies and manners during the negotiations unless you can predict with deadly accuracy the results of rigidly adversarial behavior such as showing anger or open belligerence. The ability to predict the behavior of others is second only to the management of it.

—Work outside formal settings when possible without disturbing trust. This is easier said than done, but is made easier when one is working with a sophisticated ratification hierarchy and an experienced and/or well-trained table team. Engaging in negotiations outside the formal setting early on, during the negotiation of ground rules, will usually preserve the necessary trust.

—Ask questions instead of making statements. A question allows the necessary "elbow room" that a statement cannot. There is little one can convey with a statement that one cannot convey with a well-planned question.

—Paraphrase your counterparts' statements. Rephrase their words into clear and simple terms. Get their agreement on these terms and on the actual words. This process will allow you to control the language of the negotiation and the language to be drafted into the final document. Do this often during the formal and informal off-the-record sessions.

—Summarize often. Get continuous confirmation of your summaries from the other side. This protects you from the other side trying to get any last-minute concessions.

—Take better notes of meetings and phone calls than the other side. Go over your team's notes until everyone on your team agrees about what transpired. Then, in session, compare your notes with the other side's. Yours will be better, and soon both teams will be relying on your notes. Whoever controls the notes controls the memory of the negotiation; whoever controls the memory controls the history. Write a summary of the points covered at the end of every meeting and after each phone call.

—"Close" on your words. If you have taken accurate notes and have made careful summaries of the discussions, you will be able to close the agreement in your own words. One job of the negotiator is to interpret to the other side's members what they have said. Get their understanding of the points covered, whether they seem important or not.

—Negotiation and signing an agreement are not the same thing as the implementation of it. If the relationship is good, implementation should be fairly routine.

—Creating a self-enforcing agreement by negotiating a mediation and/or arbitration clause is important to do during the negotiation at a time when the level of trust and communication is high. This will ensure the kind of future dispute settlement process that will not only be well-understood by the parties but used appropriately by them.

APPENDIX A
Time Line Management

Those who play chess can appreciate the necessity of dividing the learning and execution of that complex game into stages or phases. Chess is divided into the beginning game, the middle game, and the end game, which together, form a period of time (or time line) over which the game is played. Those who master chess know that without a well-thought and executed beginning game, the player will have difficulties in the development of the middle game, and may jeopardize success in the end game. If the beginning game is successfully executed, the most vulnerable pieces are protected from the attacks of the opponent while the most powerful attack pieces are free and clear to move against the opponent's pieces. A well-conceived and executed beginning game allows for a more effective middle game when the players literally enter a phase of exchanging the pieces in play. A successful middle game offers the opportunity for the end game to be almost a *fait accompli.*

The three games or phases fit into an overall time line which runs from the start of the beginning game to the finish of the end game. Opportunities are enhanced for the complex negotiating process to be better understood and therefore better managed by viewing the negotiating process as having separate phases or sections like chess.

The beginning game is a preparation phase when all tasks attendant to a negotiation are identified, and steps are planned to execute the tasks. This section also includes execution of the tasks when appropriate.

The middle game is the actual active meeting phase when the parties engage in informal and formal meetings and exchanges with postures described as adversarial rather than accommodative or cooperative. The first formal meeting divides the beginning section from the middle section.

The end game is the results phase when the parties exchange proposals in an accelerated fashion with more accommodation, a better atmosphere, and a less adversarial mood. This phase is usually the shortest and most intense, where experienced negotiators say 90 percent of the deals are struck. The end game also includes the steps necessary for acceptance of the final agreement by the negotiator's principals.

TIME LINE MANAGEMENT
IN NEGOTIATIONS*

I. THE BEGINNING GAME/PREPARATION PHASE

A. TASKS

1. Organize Preparation Phase

    a. Establish communication with hierarchy; set communication channels to be used throughout negotiation process
    b. Determine hierarchy's needs/goals
    c. Begin internal negotiations to influence goals and strategies
    d. Lower hierarchy's expectations
    e. Determine time line for preparation phase
        i.   ultimate bargaining deadline
        ii. personnel availability
        iii. resource availability
    f. Determine team's limits of authority
    g. Establish bureaucratic procedures

2. Choose/Develop Team

    a. Establish communications within team
    b. Practice team-building exercises
    c. Educate team members as to different styles of thinking
    d. Determine each member's strengths and roles
        i.   substantive experts
        ii.   procedural experts
        iii. spokesperson(s)
        iv.   media expert
        v.   corridor lobbyists
        vi.   leader/facilitator
        vii. recordkeeper/designated listener (including body language and sounds)
        viii. editor/language expert
        ix.   numbers expert
    e. Train team in the negotiation process
    f. Manage expectations of team members
    g. Balance stabilizers and destabilizers
    h. Assign preparation phase tasks to each member

3. Gather Information/Identify Data Needs

   a. For your side's position
   b. For the other side's position
   c. Collect information from contract administration history
   d. Collect financial/operating data
      i.   cost data
      ii. performance data
      iii. wage, cost, and performance data of organizations similarly situated by industry or region
   e. Identify external consultants and resources
   f. Identify alternatives to negotiating (*e.g.*, mediated negotiation, arbitration, litigation, etc.)
   g. Identify members of other team
      i.   identify possible cross-cultural communication problems
      ii. determine their relationship with their hierarchy
      iii. determine their hierarchy's/constituents' needs

4. Analyze Past Negotiations and the Implementation of Past Agreements

   a. Review past negotiations of both teams
   b. Assess past negotiations
      i.   did the team achieve what it strived for?
      ii. what procedures did it use?
      iii. evaluate strengths and weaknesses of past negotiations
   c. Develop an archive system for retention of data of past negotiations
   d. Assess the implementation of the last agreement
      i.   what issues came up in grievances or other disputes?
      ii. what items were difficult for us to comply with?
      iii. what items were difficult for the other side to comply with?

5. Identify Issues

   a. Determine negotiable and nonnegotiable items
   b. Determine "throw away" items
   c. Determine likely sticking points

6. Identify All Interested and Affected Parties

   a. Perform public relations activities to condition the workforce, the public
   b. Build outside alliance
   c. Educate interested parties

      i.   in the negotiation process
      ii. as to the team's goals
      iii. as to anticipated difficulties
      iv. to lower expectations
      v.   to avoid sabotage

7. Set Goals/Priorities

   a. Identify options for bargaining outcomes
   b. Set bottom line and/or "BATNA"
   c. Establish opening position
   d. Set strategy (what you want to have accomplished by when, desired timing of negotiations)
   e. Determine real and announced deadlines
   f. Begin contingency planning
   g. Anticipate and analyze union demands, both historical and new
   h. Prepare response to anticipated opening position of other team
   i. Reach consensus within team
   j. Receive a commitment to the bottom line from the hierarchy/constituency/ratifier
   k. Receive a commitment to the "BATNA" from the hierarchy/constituency/ratifier

8. Ensure the availability of administrative support

   a. Clerical
   b. Technical
   c. Equipment
   d. Security

9. Arrange First Meeting of Phase II

   a. Create opportunities for informal, prenegotiations meeting with other team to
      i.   avoid surprises
      ii. establish the relationship
      iii. share information (if both sides so desire)
   b. Determine with other team time and place of first meeting, who will be there, if it is to be "open" or "closed," etc.

B. POTENTIAL PROBLEMS (AND SOME SOLUTIONS)

1. Hierarchy does not give enough authority to team, gives unclear or changing instructions
   - Be flexible; create doubts in hierarchy's mind

2. Mutually inconsistent goals
   - Use consensus decision-making techniques

3. Team or hierarchy lacks experience or continuity
   - Train and educate

4. Distractions caused by other work/responsibilities
   - Manage time; delegate

5. Confusion caused by lack of procedure
   - Get strategy in force early

6. Goals continuously change because of changing input from:
   —the public
   - Do public relations work
   - Analyze the history of the relationship
   - Review past strategy meetings
   —the hierarchy
   - Improve communications with hierarchy; good salesmanship
   —a changing economic climate
   - Improve costing techniques

II. THE MIDDLE GAME/ACTIVE MEETING PHASE

A. TASKS

1. Negotiate Procedural Issues

   a. Introduce team members
   b. Make seating arrangements
   c. Set agenda for current meeting
   d. Set times and places for subsequent meetings
   e. Determine ground rules for negotiations
   f. Determine which team presents opening position first
   g. Establish how information is to be released to the media and to the public

2. Maintain Communication with Hierarchy/ratifiers/client

   a. Avoid surprises
   b. Lower expectations, cast doubt in their minds as to the viability of their own positions
   c. Maintain clear line of authority

d. Assess progress of negotiations
e. Constantly restate goals

3. Manage the Table Process

a. Distribute a written summarization of any previous meetings
b. Build trust; avoid promises/compromises you can't deliver
c. Be prepared for possible mediation, litigation, arbitration, etc.
d. Avoid surprising the other team
e. Cast doubts in the other team as to the viability of its position
f. Lower expectations
g. Isolate stumbling blocks, bypass obstacles—go on to other items
h. Don't let members "talk out of turn" or express disagreement at the table
i. List concerns of both sides
j. Rank priorities of both sides
k. Avoid unduly pressuring other team
l. Maintain physical and emotional edge (stamina, morale, and confidence) by taking breaks, getting a "change of scene," and caucusing
m. Keep communication with experts open (if they are not sitting on the team)
n. Listen!
o. Constantly frame questions regarding other team's proposals
p. Remain faithful to goals
q. Keep negotiations on track
r. Maintain tactical flexibility; remain open to new possibilities
s. Make "If...then..." proposals
t. Identify allies on other team
u. Identify those on other team who are resistive to your approaches and design specific responses to create doubt in their minds
v. Identify the perceptions and assumptions underlying the other team's positions
w. Don't let negotiations move too quickly or get bogged down
x. Take notes on both sides' evolving positions
y. Clarify; constantly restate all agreements so far, constantly paraphrase other team's statements and positions
z. Constantly check with data base; analyze proposals
aa. Take time to thoroughly explain positions

4. Accomplish

a. Determine if and when closure might be reached

    b. Exchange proposals and responses
    c. Exchange information
    d. Educate the other team
    e. Air feelings (and allow other side to do the same) on items not to be negotiated (to facilitate a good, ongoing relationship)

5. The Caucus

    a. Maintain sight of goals by constantly restating them
    b. Cast doubt in stabilizers' and destabilizers' minds
    c. Manage expectations
    d. Educate the other team
    e. Analyze and react to other side's proposals
    f. Assess the other side's reactions to your proposals
    g. Control internal tensions
    h. Plan strategies
    i. Control the stabilizers and destabilizers

6. The Sidebar Meeting

    a. Be honest, be yourself
    b. Don't surprise own team members—don't commit without first talking with them—promise only to recommend to your team; do not promise to act!

7. Prepare for Closing Phase

    a. Establish timing and tactics for approaching end game
    b. Avoid pushing for closure prematurely
    c. Determine format of agreement

B. *POTENTIAL PROBLEMS (AND SOME SOLUTIONS)*

1. If surprised by other team
    • Caucus

2. Other team is unreadable
    • Have a "walk-in-the-woods" session (an informal, off-the-record, relaxed and private meeting); use a series of true/false or yes/no questions

3. Growth of number of issues
    • Remember the four "ings": clustering, dropping, giving, linking

4. Other side changes positions or lacks preparation
   - Be patient; suggest a caucus

5. Other side or your side inflexible
   - Mediate or call in an outside mediator

6. Poor communication with hierarchy; hierarchy changes goals, instructions; hierarchy limits team's authority
   - Reeducate, refocus

7. Lack of discipline within team; destabilizers
   - Confront; replace; use peer pressure; create doubts

8. Failure to address counterpart's needs
   - Listen and ask questions; sidebar meeting between chief spokespersons

9. Team's strategy undercut by hierarchy's posturing for public opinion concerns
   - Use outside pressure (alliances with interest groups)

10. Information leaks
    - Improve security

11. Lack of agreement on ground rules
    - Sidebar meeting between chief spokespersons; group together items teams can agree on; compromise

12. High expectations on both sides
    - Identify assumptions/perceptions, frame questions to seed doubt

13. Misconceptions
    - Explain facts, data, and cost analyses

14. Teams do not listen to each other
    - Build trust, be consistent, and fair; ask questions of the other team at the table and of own team in caucus

15. Difficulty maintaining unified purpose and approach, both within the team and with the hierarchy
    - Promote ongoing communications

III. THE END GAME/CLOSING PHASE

A. TASKS

1. Maintain Control During Period of Accelerated "Horse Trading"

   a. Identify and prioritize major unresolved issues, which are likely to be (in labor negotiations)
      i.   economic issues (wages and benefits)
      ii. work rules (union jurisdiction and overtime scheduling)
      iii. grievance procedure
      iv. workforce flexibility
   b. Update the bottom line/BATNA
   c. Assess likelihood of other team coming to an agreement above own team's bottom line
   d. Carefully analyze possible ramifications of any changes in positions at this time
   e. Execute appropriate contingencies
   f. Maintain especially good (and quick) communication channels with hierarchy
   g. Continue public relations work with various constituencies
   h. Take careful, accurate notes
   i. Maintain a united front
   j. Predetermine a possible eleventh-hour dispute resolution mechanism if not agreed to during ground rule discussions
   k. Negotiate an implementation mechanism for the agreement
   l. Determine who will draft the agreement
   m. Determine how the agreement will be announced to the public and by whom
   n. Ensure administrative support availability

2. Monitor Activity of Other Team

   a. With the press
   b. In current problems or disputes

3. Come to Verbal Agreement
   a. Ensure agreement is within position
   b. Confirm that all parties understand proposed agreement

4. Sell the Agreement to All Concerned Parties
   a. Use other team's arguments to sell agreement to
      i.   destabilizers

      ii. hierarchy
      iii. constituents
      iv. outside interests
   b. Get as much as possible for your potential "losers"

5. Draft the Agreement
   a. Allow opportunity for comment, revision
   b. Check every draft with team in caucus
   c. Reconfirm with experts/data base
   d. Reconfirm with hierarchy/ratifiers
   e. Reconfirm terms and language with the other team on and off the record

6. Close
   a. Sign the agreement
   b. Observe any traditional ceremony/protocol
   c. Publicize the agreement
   d. Celebrate in an appropriate manner

B. POTENTIAL PROBLEMS (AND SOME SOLUTIONS)

1. Last-ditch efforts by destabilizers
   - Educate destabilizers as to the cost of not closing

2. Attempts by other side to reopen issues already settled or to introduce new issues
   - Establish ground rules to prevent introduction of new issues after designated cutoff

3. Stabilizers too anxious to close
   - Remind them of wishes of constituents/hierarchy/ratifiers/closers

4. Agreement has gone beyond a position acceptable to constituents/hierarchy/ratifiers/closers
   - Sidebar meeting

5. Change in external factors makes agreement untenable
   - Bring in a mediator

6. One side gets ratification, other side does not
   - Establish (through negotiations) a dispute settlement mechanism

7. Hierarchy enters the negotiations
   - Get the two hierarchies together (if they are educated/
     experienced in the negotiation process)

8. Separate agreements are reached between factions of
   both teams
   - Control own team

9. Hierarchy continues to insist on unrealistic goals
   - Generate outside pressure on hierarchy to accept agreement

10. Time constraints
    - Identify managers authorized to make decisions at critical times

11. Breakdown of team spirit
    - Periodic briefing of team members as to generalities and details

12. Negotiations over contract language continue after the
    formal table negotiations end
    - Write language as articles are agreed to

13. Too many layers of authority in the negotiations
    - Grant chief spokesperson more authority

---

* Prepared for the American Arbitration Association by Alison Lobb.

On Mediation

The following piece titled "On Mediation" was developed in 1989 in response to a request for American Arbitration Association skill training for new mediators for the Independent Mediation Service of South Africa (IMSSA), which is an independent dispute resolution organization funded by the Ford Foundation and the British and other governments. Specifically, the purpose of the piece was to provide "mental targets" for new mediators as they progressed through the early information gathering stages of a mediated negotiation.

A negotiator needs to understand the mind-set of a mediator when involved in a mediated negotiation. This appendix can help a negotiator to "think" like a mediator when caught between factions on his or her team or when it is necessary to mediate between negotiators and their ratifiers and with their counterparts across the table. The professional negotiator knows how to mediate.

ON MEDIATION

Since mediation is an extension of the negotiation process, what should a mediator consider when he or she steps into the process?

- Issues
- Wants of the parties
- Needs of the parties
- Proposals of the parties
- Positions of the parties
- Interests of the parties—"Getting to Yes" *
- Stakes of the parties
- Expectations:
    What the advocates expect of themselves
    What the advocates expect of each other
    What the closers/clients expect of their advocates
    What the closers/clients expect of the opposing advocates
        and opposing closers/clients
    What the advocates expect of the negotiation process
    What the advocates expect of a mediator
    What the advocates expect of a specific mediation in a
        specific negotiation
- The degree of trust that exists:
    Across the table
    Within each negotiation team
    Between the team and the closers
    Among the closers/clients/ratifiers
- "Facts" as agreed to by the parties
- Assumptions of the parties
- "Politics" of the situation (inside and outside)
- Outside factors impacting on the negotiation
- Negotiation ground rules
- Law of the sector
- Power relationship and the criteria used by the parties
  to establish the power equities
- History of the relationship: Is this a one-shot negotiation
  or part of a long-term relationship?
- Goal of the parties
- Strategies of the parties
- Objectives of the parties
- Tactics of the parties
- Purpose: to resolve a dispute? avoid a dispute? solve a prob-

lem? harmonize a relationship? improve a relationship?

- BATNAs** of the parties
- Intentions of the parties
- Perceptions of the parties
- Sophistication of the parties
- Drafting skills of the parties
- Length of the "leash" between negotiator/advocate and closer/client
- Resources of the parties: legal, technical, political, financial
- Degree of desperation of parties
- Ability to prevail in an evidentiary process as perceived by the parties
- Perception of willingness to go to trial
- Personalities of the advocates and their styles of convincing and being convinced (idealists, realists, pragmatists, synthesists, analysts)
- What is the degree of paranoia?
- Compulsory vs. voluntary mediation
- Best alternative process to a negotiated settlement: hearing, court, arbitration, med/arb, fact-finding, etc.
- What does the passage of time do to the interests of the parties?
- What does the passage of time do to the expectations of the parties?
- How the role of a mediator is defined by the negotiation
- What is "just" according to the parties?
- What is "fair" according to the parties?
- What is "equitable" according to the parties?
- What is "truth" according to the parties?

---

* By authors Roger Fisher and William Ury in *Getting To Yes*
** BATNA—Best Alternative To a Negotiated Agreement

Styles of Persuasion

By Renelle Rae

As we learn more about the negotiation process it becomes clear that one's effectiveness as a negotiator (and mediator) is centered on the ability to convince, to persuade, and to influence others—in other words, to create doubt and uncertainty in others' minds as to the viability of their positions, interests, and expectations. As noted earlier in this book, you can not create doubt without first creating trust. Someone who does not trust you will not allow you to create doubt!

Intuitively, we attempt to convince others in the same way we like to be convinced, but we also realize that not everyone thinks the way we do. For this reason, we should consider expanding our styles of persuasion in order to be more effective. The information in the following appendix will afford you an opportunity to understand more about yourself and other people and how to convince those who think differently. This will increase your negotiation power.

The following article is adapted from a presentation developed by Renelle Rae who bases her premises on the 1977 book, *The Art of Thinking* (rereleased in 1982 as *The Styles of Thinking*) by Bramson and Harrison.

Ms. Rae, director of career development at the U. S. Environmental Protection Agency (EPA), is an attorney and has designed and conducted courses on negotiation, trial advocacy, and environmental law for various government organizations. Her training expertise covers management, human relations and effective speaking.

STYLES OF PERSUASION

Persuasion is a fundamental part of the negotiation process. A negotiator's ability to convey information and ideas to others is crucial. If people cannot understand your ideas, how can they be persuaded? In *The Art of Thinking* the Style of Thinking InQ Profile is a test that can be used to help people understand the way they process information to arrive at a decision. Once they answer the questions, they realize that there are very different, but equally valid ways to process information and reach decisions that will:

1. help them think more strategically about how to communicate ideas to others;
2. lower their annoyance level when dealing with people with different thinking styles, and to help them understand why they become irritated with people who have different approaches;
3. improve their understanding of team dynamics and how to work better in teams.

A person's thinking style has an impact on each member in a negotiation. The best way to describe this influence is to use the analogy of communication through "stencils." Our stencil is our individual perception of the world. It dominates how we discern situations, what information we allow into our thought process, and how we permit ourselves to be influenced by others. Since birth, we have been bombarded with a tremendous amount of data that we absorbed through our five senses and our intuition. We processed this information to understand the world, but quickly learned that sensory overload would result if we tried to register all the information hurled at us. Instead, we learned to filter information by retaining some and ignoring the rest; we decide what is important to us.

If you are dealing with someone who has a similar stencil, it is likely that person will freely accept your idea. Your information is likely to easily sail through the holes in his or her stencil and have impact. When a person's stencil is very different from yours, the holes you have in common are much narrower, and your theories may not register. You may feel that the person is rejecting your ideas because they are unacceptable, when in actuality it is your concept or approach that is misunderstood.

Bramson and Harrison's InQ Questionnaire refers to five categories of thinkers: the synthesist, the idealist, the pragmatist, the analyst, and the realist. The test can be used to help negotiators improve the way they communicate their ideas and influence others. It tends to pigeonhole people into one of the five categories or a combination of them. Some people may feel uncomfortable with this process. However, in order to think strategically on how to influence others, it is necessary to define the key categories (stencils) of thinking and to describe how one category differs from another.

You may blend several styles of thinking or you may have one dominant mode of processing information. People who have more than one style may experience some internal debate about the best way to approach a situation. But they also tend to view the problem from different angles. Followers of this "chameleon" approach to thinking solve problems situationally. Thus, it is difficult to predict how to influence them.

One-stylers are easier to predict. However, there is a danger in assuming that anyone's behavior can be predicted. If you find yourself reacting negatively or you have difficulty communicating, it may be due to differences in your styles of thinking.

The five different styles of thinkers and their approaches to problem solving should give you clues on identifying a person's style, recognizing the strengths and weaknesses that style brings to the negotiation process, and ways to influence the person.

The Synthesist

Synthesists comprise 11% of the population, the smallest percentage of all thinking styles. The synthesist perceives a world of conflict in which ideas, people, and concepts are constantly clashing. Conflict is viewed as productive because out of the clash of ideas comes something new and better than the original thought. Sometimes a synthesist will engage in conflict as a devil's advocate to test the soundness of a solution. At times the synthesist enjoys being a third party observer watching people debate an issue after having launched the grenade that initiated the discussion.

Before making a decision, a synthesist likes to view the problem from as many different angles as possible. The synthesist has a need to understand the world, but not necessarily to control it. The synthesist style is more speculative and theoretical than the other styles in terms of collecting a lot of information and asking many "What if" questions. The synthesist's speculation sometimes goes a little too far beyond the daily realities of the other styles, but these different perspectives and questions enable the person to be more outrageously inventive than the other styles. The questioning of assumptions and the devil's advocate approach on the long-term consequences of a negotiated solution can lead to more solid, successfully implemented solutions.

A synthesist may find it difficult to stop speculating about alternatives in the close phase of the negotiation process and commit to implementing one solution. The confrontational nature of the synthesist approach may create a feeling of low trust or bad rapport in a non-synthesist unless that party understands the synthesist's use of conflict as a means to get to higher quality solutions.

The strength of the synthesist's style in negotiating is that he or she rarely takes anything at face value. Tom Colosi, in his thoughts about the job of a negotiator, talks about the need to create doubts in another person's mind about the viability of his or her position. The synthesist excels at probing for underlying assumptions and transcending the face value of any assertion. Other thinking styles may have a dominant currency for persuading people, but a synthesist responds by questioning why you are giving your facts or theory or value. The synthesist wants to know what assumptions you are making and what your hidden agenda is. This can be extremely annoying to people who are not synthesist thinkers. If you ask a synthesist a question, you may get a question in return.

The synthesist's desire to be a devil's advocate is an asset in negotiating, but it is important to know when to play that role. Developing creative solutions requires a green light/red light process. The green light process is a time of brainstorming when all members of the group cast their ideas. In the red light phase, the ideas are critiqued for short- and long-term implications. When you brainstorm with a synthesist, the solutions offered by others may be challenged (red lighted) immediately, and the group may have a difficult time getting to a flowing green light stage. At the beginning of any brainstorming process, it is important to negotiate the ground rule which includes postponing the red light critic until the green light process has produced the best possible solution.

Sometimes a synthesist's proposals are too theoretical or abstract to meet the immediacy of a fast-paced negotiation. It is important to get the synthesist to phrase solutions in less abstract terms. Use any cajoling needed to bring the person down to reality. "That's an interesting suggestion. Can you give us a specific example of how it would work in this situation?" A synthesist may bounce from topic to topic. For the synthesist this is a creative process, but other styles of thinkers get lost as the synthesist moves around. Once again, cajole the synthesist to keep focused on the solutions at hand.

The synthesist is the most difficult of all thinkers to influence, having a need to remain independent and unpersuaded by the group until the speculative, devil's advocate process is complete. Here is a tip: Be prepared to participate in a lively debate in which the synthesist may switch over to your side and expect you to reciprocate. This desire to see a problem from the other person's perspective is an asset in negotiating mutually satisfactory settlements.

The Idealist

The idealist is the most common style of thinker, comprising 37% of the population. The idealist's world is harmonious, focusing on people rather than things. The idealist believes that everything in the world is connected to everything else like interlocking gears and that one problem cannot be fixed without the solution having an impact on something else. When an idealist problem solves, there may be trouble figuring out where to begin and which part of the problem to tackle first. Sometimes the approaches of other styles are needed to help the idealist take the first step toward a solution.

The idealist tries to find a way to harmonize all views by making goals broad and focusing on the smallest area of agreement. An idealist begins problem solving in groups trying to establish a unifying point where everyone can agree.

Being more tuned into the people side of the problem, the idealist demonstrates empathetic and receptive behavior to others, even opponents. An idealist will often nod and smile to make the other person feel comfortable, but beware of head nodding; it does not necessarily signify agreement or an emotional commitment to implement the agreement. Emotional commitment will come only when an idealist has decided to trust you and feels that the agreement is the right and most advantageous thing to do. While the idealist does not ask for reciprocity, there is some expectation that the other side will at least be interested in hearing the points of contention, and will be offended if that interest is not shown.

The idealist focuses on building the relationship and trust with opponents before starting negotiations. Also, the idealist tends to take time up front to negotiate an overall goal with the home team and with the other side. This goal can be a tremendous asset later in the negotiation when both sides reach an impasse. The focus on relationships and overall goals provides maximum benefit in negotiations that require long-term implementation. The idealist excels in emotional, unstructured, value-laden negotiations in which an objective, detached problem-solving approach will not work.

A key liability of the idealist is the distrust of hard data in negotiating. Yet, solutions must sound technically viable as well as be amenable to the people. The idealist sometimes overlooks the technical aspect.

Decision making is an assimilative process for the idealist. Everybody's views should be heard, and everybody should get a little of something they need. The idealist struggles for the perfect negotiated solution. The negotiation process, driven by deadlines, rarely offers enough time for perfecting the compromised solution.

To influence an idealist, avoid conflict at all cost. This style does not deal well with pushy people who make demands. An idealist may not take on the demanding person directly, but probably will dig in and refuse to budge. Passive-aggressiveness may also result from a confrontation. To avoid conflict, the idealist may go along and close the deal, but may not complete the bargain when it comes to implementation.

The best way to enlist an idealist's support is to ask for help. Asking, "Can you help me with my problem?" will be more appreciated by an idealist than speaking in a demanding style.

You may experience passive-aggressive behavior from an idealist even though the situation is not demanding. The idealist has a strong need to please other people even when needs are not being met. To avoid passive-aggressiveness, give the idealist permission to stop being Mr. Nice Guy. The idealist must be encouraged to level with you, give you bad news, and tell you things that might hurt your feelings. It is important to persuade the idealist to reveal negative perceptions about the deal.

The negative contingency diagram approach is a useful tool in getting the idealist to speak openly with you. This is an exercise in which the group brainstorms from a negative or devil's advocate point of view. You may ask the group, "How can we ruin this solution or its implementation?" Each member has permission to suggest negative things.

The best way to enlist an idealist's support is to ask for help. Be sure to speak in terms of people and subject values. An idealist may begin to distrust you if you throw around a lot of numbers or focus on costs. You need to know what the impact of those numbers is on the people and the organization's morale. Do they have the ability to reach some overall subject goal that the idealist envisions? If you are at a loss as to what information to provide, ask the idealist what it will take to be persuasive. Of all the thinking styles, the idealist is bound to openly reveal personal needs.

The idealist must be gently encouraged towards a final decision. This style strives to meet high standards, and doesn't encourage the surrender of options. Let the idealist know that you understand the concern for the people side of the problem, and coach and gently nudge toward a decision.

The Pragmatist

The pragmatists, making up 18% of the population, view the world as chaotic and unpredictable. There is no use in long-term planning because Murphy's Law is always lying in wait to upset any order. The pragmatist has high energy and is an enthusiastic, experimental type who approaches problem solving by jumping right in, zigzagging through a problem with short-term plans, gathering information needed to solve it. They look for the shortest route to a payoff.

This type of thinker's short-term style can lead the person to run into pitfalls which are usually transcended by relying on several generic contingency plans to overcome problems. In addition to these plans, the pragmatist uses finely tuned people skills to get assistance. Enlisting the help of others is a specialty. This short-term focus and reliance on generic contingency plans usually helps the pragmatist reach the payoff quicker than is achieved through other thinking styles. The short-term approach is reinforced over and over again.

Since the pragmatist expects Murphy's Law to foil any carefully made plans, little time is wasted planning. Instead, contingency methods are perfected. Consistency of concepts, theories, and methods are of little interest to a pragmatist; the method that works in each individual situation is swiftly adopted. Tomorrow a different method might work better. Others may accuse the pragmatist of being shallow or opportunist. They resent the pragmatist's lack of concern for consistency.

Flexibility is a key asset of the pragmatist in negotiating. Pragmatism is the most adaptable of all the styles. The pragmatist will abandon an unproductive strategy and rely on one of many contingency plans if the plans of the other styles are not working. Negotiation teams often experience tension when trying to decide when to abandon an unproductive strategy. The pragmatist has the ability to help team members when they get paralyzed in the planning stage.

The pragmatist's ability to market ideas and win support is useful in the negotiation process. However, while an immediate rapport may develop with someone a pragmatist sometimes has problems gaining the person's trust because of appearing inconsistent in the arguments made on a position. Other styles may wonder about the pragmatist's ability to stay committed to a deal.

The tendency to ignore the long-term consequences of a decision is a liability of the pragmatist. The short-term focus makes it difficult to avoid going off on tangents and staying with the long-term plan.

The pragmatist is the easiest of all the thinkers to influence. Present a great sales pitch, and the pragmatist will march along behind you. That's good news, but you must realize that the next person who comes along with a better sales pitch might persuade the pragmatist to go along with him or her. To keep a pragmatist on your side, you have to persistently reinforce his or her commitment to you.

Have fun with the pragmatist as you tackle problems together. When negotiating, the pragmatist has a need to be playful and experimental and does not relate well with styles that are heavy and laborious in problem solving. The group can accomplish its job as well as have a good time. Often the pragmatist will crack jokes to give the group energy or to dispel tension.

You must realize that the pragmatist has a tendency toward passive-aggressiveness since challenging opponents is avoided. The pragmatist wants to gather support, so negative aspects about another's approach may be concealed. Use the contingency diagram to discover these negative thoughts.

Perhaps the most important thing to remember when trying to influence a pragmatist is to use your selling powers; give a marketing pitch. Be creative and playful. If you have a pragmatist on your team, give that person the job of taking the proposed solution and giving it a marketing slant. The pragmatist instinctively knows what sells, so harness that talent.

The Analyst

The analyst thinker, who sees the world as structured, organized and predictable, comprises 35% of the population. This powerful mind focuses on logic and organization. Even when Murphy's Law foils an analyst's carefully structured plan, the belief remains that the world "should" be organized and predictable.

The analyst has a formula for making decisions that uses a deductive process. The first step is to look for a governing method, theory or premise that will guide the process. Once the right method is found, it is implemented by collecting relevant data, developing alternative solutions, and conducting a pro/con analysis of the proposed solutions to arrive at the one best way to solve the problem.

The analyst loves detail and organizing information. Giving and receiving voluminous amounts of detail is one of the ways an analyst demonstrates competency. It is also a way the analyst checks other styles for their competency and trustworthiness.

In negotiating, the analyst is able to provide stability and structure to the planning process by advocating a systematic evaluation of alternatives before a decision is made on a negotiation strategy or a bottom line. Proposals are designed with logic and rationality and with great attention to the accuracy of the details provided to support any position.

Once an analyst has decided on a strategy, the decision to close on a deal will not be made until all the consequences have been evaluated.

Of all the styles of thinking, the analyst has the best understanding and ability to do complete staff work. Completed projects are picture perfect. However, this perfection is demanded from peers as well, and low tolerance for incomplete work can become a liability.

Successful negotiating requires the ability to master both substantive issues and personal issues in a case. Sometimes the analyst fails to build the relationships and trust needed to work through the more difficult substantive issues. When an analyst tries to deal with emotional issues through the scientific, deductive method, the person with the emotional issue may be alienated.

An analyst may be perceived by other styles as inflexible and overly cautious. Often the negotiation process, driven by a deadline, does not allow the analyst enough time to complete the problem-solving process. If the analyst is forced by others to make a decision too quickly, the analyst may become passive-aggressive in the implementation phase. The lack of adequate time can make the analyst hold firm to a position and become a destabilizer, which leads to an impasse.

It is very difficult to change an analyst's mind after it is focused on the one best way to solve a problem. Other thinking styles need to muster all their ammunition and proceed to attack the analyst's decision; usually the analyst does not budge. The analyst often doubts the decision-making processes used by other styles.

To be successful in persuading the analyst you need to listen to details. Do not interrupt; your competency will come into question if you are not interested in details. When you relate your own details, be sure to be accurate, particularly with numbers.

To influence an analyst, do not waste time attacking conclusions. Instead, go back to the beginning of the person's decision-making process. Look for any erroneous assumptions or flaws in the method used. An analyst takes pride in being rational, accurate, and competent at all times. If you discover an inaccuracy in theory or inconsistency in rationale, the analyst's desire to show competency will force the person to reconsider the problem with your new information.

To impress an analyst, do your homework. Check all your details and strive for logic and accuracy. Present information in a systematic and organized manner. Your interest in the accuracy of the details is a key measure for the analyst in deciding whether to trust you.

To change an analyst's mind, look for the theory that governs the data to be collected. Search for the paradigm that structures the analyst's world and prevents the person from accepting other solutions. Create doubts through logic and deduction that the paradigm is the only viable one.

Do not be bothered by what Bramson and Harrison call "the great stone face" of the analyst. This thinking style gives the least verbal and nonverbal feedback. An analyst will listen intently, giving little acknowledgment to you or your ideas, checking you for accuracy and competency. Do not panic. Continue providing the analyst with information in a systematic manner, but check in every now and then. In some cases, the most feedback you will get from an analyst is a grunt, but a conscientious one will reward you with a brilliant, logical restatement of your theories at the end.

The Realist

The realist—24% of the population—is assertive and action oriented and views the world through the limits of experience. The realist's world is comprised of the knowledge gathered through the senses of sight, hearing, scent, taste, and touch. If a realist has not experienced a thing, then it does not exist. Conversely, a realist expects everyone else to recognize the validity of the realist's personal experiences. In addition to personal experiences, a realist will accept information from "experts."

A realist's focus is on the decision-making process, not necessarily on the quality of the final decision, preferring to fix things and move on. A realist will make a decision without additional information or evaluation if there is enough empirical information to solve it. One good solution is enough to satisfy a realist.

Confident about the world and the realistic decision-making process, a realist will expect others to be equally sure about their views. But since most other thinkers need additional information before taking action, they tend to be less confident than the realist. If a person hesitates in responding the realist assumes that the person does not know what to do. This compels the realist to take charge.

The realist style is an incisive style. These people do not waste time with small talk, rather they cut through the rhetoric and get things done. They are usually direct, and their words often have a corrective quality. With a realist, you do not have to worry about passive-aggressiveness. Rather, you need to have a thick skin and not get defensive. With a realist, you always know where you stand.

A realist's strength is a focus on the realities of the current situation, resources, and the bottom line, keeping the negotiation on track and reminding everyone of deadlines. A realist provides drive and momentum by asking the tough questions like, "Can we do this?" and "What will fix this problem?"

If a realist pushes too hard for closure, other styles may be destabilized because they have not been allowed to work through their decision-making processes. In the realist's eagerness to reach a decision, the person sometimes may have trouble recognizing disagreement on either side. Trivial issues to a realist may be really important to another person.

To influence a realist, provide the facts, and make your statement brief. Act secure in your views even if you need more information to feel truly confident. To keep the attention of the realist, begin with the bottom line solution. Be assertive, and state your case like this: "This is what we should do. This is why and this is what is in it for you."

Do not try to surprise a realist, since surprise can result in defensiveness and unproductive problem solving. Give a realist the feeling of control when you make proposals.

You can persuade a realist by planting your idea and letting the realist take credit for it. The realist engages in appropriation. For example, when a realist reads a book, information becomes the realist's own. If the realist does not view you as an expert, your data may be rejected. In this case, enlist the help of a person who the realist will trust as an expert.

Be firm, but be fair. Stand up for your views. Present your positions with conviction and be prepared for a factual debate. In the end you may have to agree to disagree over the absolute truth of any fact, but design a negotiated solution that corrects the problem.

INFLUENCING OTHERS

Cardinal Rule of Influencing
- Never threaten another person's sense of
  —Importance
  —Competency
  —Acceptance

SYNTHESISTS
- They are the hardest to influence because they like conflict.
- Let them reinvent the wheel if they want!
- Keep them focused on the problem at hand.
- Tap their inventive talents by brainstorming.

IDEALISTS
- They appeal to high values and standards.
- Ask, "Can you help me with my problem?"

- Help them to not be too nice.
- Nudge them gently toward a decision.
- Avoid conflict.

PRAGMATISTS
- Have fun with them. Don't take yourself too seriously.
- Be experimental.
- Playfully negotiate the win/win solution—everything is a tradeoff.
- Let them feel well-liked.
- Help them to be candid.
- Take a marketing stance.

ANALYSTS
- Meet them on their own ground. Plan and present your case like an analyst.
- Do your homework.
- Be meticulous and accurate.
- Do not be confused by their lack of feedback.
- Do not get swamped by their data.
- Look for the theoretical base they rest their case on.

REALISTS
- Get their attention by acting like a realist—strong and incisive.
- Get to your point quickly.
- Be firm but fair.
- Let them have control.
- Encourage appropriation.
- Do not surprise them.

An edited summary by Renelle Rae from Bramson and Harrison's *The Art of Thinking*, 1977.

The Iceberg Principle: Secrecy in Negotiation

The following article by Thomas Colosi is edited and adapted from the book, *Perspectives on Negotiation: Four Case Studies and Interpretations*, published by the Department of State Publication Foreign Service Institute Center for the Study of Foreign Affairs in January 1986.

CHARACTERISTICS OF NEGOTIATION

In an article from the August 18,1985, issue of the *New York Times Magazine* titled "The PLO in Exile," Judith Miller wrote:

> On a crisp day last February (1985), a small group of men, once bitter enemies, sat around King Hussein's dining room table in the Nadwa Palace, in the Jordanian capital of Amman.
>
> They had argued for weeks over the document they had drafted, over weighty issues that sometimes hinged on the addition of a word, the deletion of a comma. At several points, Yasir Arafat, chairman of the Palestine Liberation Organization, had threatened to abandon the effort. At other times, Hussein had indicated, he wanted Arafat to leave.
>
> But finally, after two months of *secret* (emphasis added) meetings, they reached agreement. Jordan and the PLO, 15 years after their bloody civil war, devised an accord outlining the principles of a joint bid for peace with Israel.
>
> The agreement, announced February 11, was a milestone. For the first time ever, the PLO's leadership accepted the notion of a negotiated solution to the Arab-Israeli crisis—without mentioning armed struggle. For the first time it appeared to relinquish its claim to an independent Palestinian state in favor of a state federated with Jordan, and committed itself to being part of a joint Jordanian-Palestinian delegation at new Middle East peace talks.
>
> For the first time, too, the PLO had endorsed all United Nations Security Council resolutions dealing with the Arab-Israeli conflict, including, implicitly, Resolution 242, which recognizes Israel's right to exist "within secure and recognized borders" in exchange for return of the territories that Israel has occupied since the 1967 war.
>
> Arafat has not explicitly endorsed U.N. Resolution 242. But neither did he object when Hussein, visiting the United Nations last May, insisted that the PLO had accepted that resolution. Arafat's silence has thus been widely construed as affirmation.

The article continues to chronicle events leading to the February 1985 meeting, and attempts to analyze the implications of this momentous event with such important opportunities and problems involving all parties concerned.

We can only analyze information we are allowed to know, and, in any given negotiation, this information is controlled by the parties, either jointly or severally, and usually by mutual agreement. The negotiating parties seek to manage not only the substantive aspects of the negotiation and all parts of the negotiated solution (assuming there is one), but also the process through which the solution is reached. In her article, Ms. Miller was hampered by the same obstacles of analysis and evaluation faced by me and others writing on case studies: privacy and secrecy, two necessary characteristics of the negotiation and mediation processes. The more difficult the negotiation, the greater the perceived need for privacy and secrecy.

I call this the "Iceberg Principle": a negotiation is analogous to an iceberg in that we are allowed to see only one-tenth of it. Negotiators usually keep private nine-tenths of what really happens in a difficult negotiation.

Some Fundamentals of Negotiation

1. The negotiation process is a decision-making process.

2. The essence of a negotiation is that it provides opportunities for the parties to exchange commitments or promises through which they resolve their disagreements and reach a settlement.

3. Ninety percent of the negotiation takes place in the last 10% of the time allowed, emphasizing the importance of a mutually credible deadline.

4. The negotiation process, except in U.S. labor relations law, has few procedural rules, but procedure is as much a product of negotiation as the substantive issues and is, of course, negotiable.

5. Goal, strategy, objectives, and tactics are situational.

6. In the vast majority of negotiations the lion (stronger party) will get the lion's share, and the lamb (weaker party) will get the lamb's share, assuming there is a shared criteria for strength and weakness. It is rare that parties to a negotiation have equal power. Sometimes, however, strength is a matter of perception: If one party perceives the other as the lion, the other party is the lion for that particular negotiation.

7. Negotiators mediate and mediators negotiate.

8. Parties to a negotiation may agree to the same solution for entirely different reasons.

9. Parties to a negotiation are not only those negotiating "across the table" (horizontally); parties also negotiate within the team at the table or in caucus. Negotiations occur between the "table

team members" and their respective decision makers (ratifiers) and also within the ratifiers as they attempt to decide upon the team's directions. A three-party negotiation is not just arithmetically or geometrically more complex than a two-party model; two of the parties may agree on a particular issue and disagree with the third party, while on other issues the parties may change allegiances depending on the issue...and so on.

Communicating and Creating Trust

10. Parties to a negotiation will find it difficult, if not impossible, to exchange promises or commitments with each other if they do not trust each other to deliver on the promise or commitment.

11. When trust is low or nonexistent in a relationship, the parties find it difficult to reveal their expectations.

12. When communication is problematic in a relationship, parties do not listen effectively to each other. Ineffective listening due to poor communication creates problems in understanding.

13. When effective listening is absent or weak in a relationship, it is not possible for each side to educate the other as to its interests and the viability of its positions. That kind of education is one of the most constructive activities of negotiation.

14. When it is allowed to occur within the context of a negotiation, education is the most important way for the expectations of the negotiating parties to be managed or lowered. Understanding the equation between expectations and proposals is critical to bargaining in a negotiation. If an expectation cannot be lowered, a proposal that fails to meet that expectation is either rejected or accepted reluctantly, causing one to assume difficulties in the implementation of the agreement. If the expectations can be learned and understood, an opportunity is afforded either to raise the proposal to meet that expectation or to work to lower the expectation within the proposal range or both.

Creating Doubts and Uncertainties

15. The basic job of all negotiators is to create doubts and uncertainties in the minds of others as to the viability of their positions if the parties do not agree with the negotiator. Doubt creation is central to the art of persuasion. It is either a positive or negative act, depending on the intent of the party. The best way to create doubts is through education (if others are listening). If

the other parties agree, the negotiator can relax and focus on reducing verbal promises and commitments to writing (this usually involves a second negotiation).

When there is a disagreement, the negotiator tries to elicit a behavioral change from the other party (whether "the other party" sits at the table on the negotiator's own team or is the negotiator's ratification authority). The behavioral change eventually coincides with the negotiator's approach or position. This behavioral change is indicated by a change in proposal or by presentation of a new counterproposal.

16. Before a party changes its behavior, it must change its mind-set. Prior to a change in mind-set it must doubt its mind-set. If the party's own team (with all its factions) or its own ratification authority (with all its factions) cannot create sufficient doubts in the minds of the negotiators to cause them to change their proposal to harmonize with the other party, then it is the negotiator's job to create those doubts and uncertainties to initiate the chain of change from modification of mind-set, to counterproposal and then to agreement.

17. Negotiators must instill trust and confidence in the minds of others to provide a basis for creating doubts and uncertainties.

18. The most effective way for negotiators to create trust and confidence is to be themselves, since many of the most difficult negotiations are handled through a one-on-one meeting by two people with some degree of trust in each other.

Facts and Nonfacts

19. Negotiators create both "facts" and "nonfacts" by mutual agreement. In negotiation, an unchallenged assumption usually becomes a "fact" for that particular negotiation. That explains why secrecy is essential in the conduct of many difficult negotiations. Assuming settlement, the parties then concentrate on how to explain the "facts" and "nonfacts" in an acceptable way to others.

20. In a trial (court/administrative law procedure/arbitration) the basic job of an attorney as well as a nonlawyer/advocate in an arbitration is to create doubts, by any quantum of proof necessary, in the mind of the third party decider-of-fact (judge, jury, ALJ, arbitrator) as to the viability of the other advocate's position in the case. In a trial, advocates are limited to supporting their theories by offering their perceptions of facts supported by evidence that the advocates hope the third party decider-of-fact will accept.

In the negotiation process, however, the deciders-of-fact sit across the table from each other. While trial procedure is fact-oriented in an effort to establish "the truth of the matter," in a negotiation process the truth is whatever the negotiators agree it is. Negotiators may take scientifically, legally or historically provable facts and render them "non-facts" if they create problems for the negotiators as they attempt to settle their dispute. If negotiators disagree among themselves as to what constitutes a certain fact, then for those negotiators that "fact" is not accepted as such.

21. Since many disciplines rely on facts for decision making, the consternation and frustration of individuals who base decision making on scientifically and legally created logic is understandable. In a negotiation, decisions are reached not so much on legal, scientific or historical grounds as generally understood, but rather on "facts" as the negotiators understand and perceive them.

The Importance of Privacy

22. Since negotiators rely on their own perceptions and mutual agreement with their opposites to establish "facts" in support of their decisions, they have a profound need for privacy. Nearly 80% of the cases filed for suit in the United States are not adjudicated by a judge and jury, but are settled out of court without unnecessary public disclosure, emphasizing the importance of privacy in this process even in legal negotiations. The large number of grievance settlements through labor relations and of insurance claims adjusted through negotiation underscores the frequency of the activity, and also the importance of privacy in the dispute settlement.

23. Since privacy is such an essential characteristic of the negotiation process, the actual events either during or after a high-stakes negotiation are seldom known. The only available information is what the negotiators reveal. Often the negotiators themselves (whether or not they are at the table) are unaware of the implications of what has happened as a result of a given negotiation over the long term.

Do we really know what happened between President John F. Kennedy and Premier Nikita Khrushchev to "negotiate" an end to the Cuban Missile Crisis and all of the long-term implications? Do we really know what promises and commitments were exchanged between the late President Anwar El-Sadat, the late Prime Minister Menachem

Begin and President Jimmy Carter to bring about the negotiated settlement referred to as the Camp David Accords? How much do we know about what really transpired in negotiations between the United States and Iran to induce the return of the 52 hostages in exchange for the utilization of the arbitration process to resolve disputes over $8 billion in alleged Iranian assets? What really occurred between the United States and the faction of Shiite Moslems in the TWA hostage negotiations? In between these "nonnegotiators" were Nabih Berri of the more conservative Shiites, the late President Hafez al-Assad of Syria, the Algerians, the governments of Israel and Iran, the Russians and perhaps others. What really occurred in the various talks among all of these parties will probably remain private for some time.

Levels of Difficulty in Negotiations

24. In an "easy" negotiation, most of the actual negotiating (exchanges of promises and commitments) takes place in a rather official way, across the table, with few matters discussed unofficially in sidebar meetings or telephone conversations away from the table. A good deal of the negotiation activity is placed on the record with little necessity for privacy.

25. In a "difficult" negotiation, less activity is placed on the record, for less actual negotiating occurs across the table, although more notification and education takes place. If the negotiation is to succeed, each party must have trust that its off-the-record agreements will be reflected as per mutual agreement on-the-record at the official negotiation. Mediation may be appropriate in this type of negotiation, with the mediator agreeing to keep off-the-record occurrences private to the parties and the mediator. In this type of negotiation, it is important to note that the parties agree on what information is to remain private and for how long, as well as what information is to be made available for public knowledge.

26. In a negotiation deemed "extremely difficult," a great deal of the actual negotiation occurs off the record by fewer people, perhaps involving mediation, with far less information available on the record for analysis. Less information is available for public interest as agreed by the parties off the record.

27. A negotiation termed "impossible" is characterized by a perception that little or no negotiating activity transpires until a breakthrough is discovered by those meeting sub rosa, which opens the door to engaging in an "extremely difficult" negotiation. If

the parties really have the will to reach agreement, the negotiation will move to a level whereby the parties begin a "difficult" negotiation with its aforementioned characteristics. Continued determination to reach a negotiated settlement offers an opportunity for the parties to move into an "easy" negotiation.

28. A negotiation at the difficult level is not static. Negotiations can be more or less difficult, depending on external and internal elements, which can include events that depose or weaken a leader to a personality problem between the principal negotiators at the table.

29. The more difficult the negotiation, the more expertise that is required of the negotiators.

Skills, Responsibilities, and Tasks of the Negotiator

- Delegator
- Understand the goal
- Set objectives
- Decide tactics
- Oversight
- Persuader (key item)
- Manage the planning
- Manage the preparation
- Spokesperson—formal (across the table) and informal (off the record)
- Technical expert
- Ability to understand expectations of the ratifier, team, counterpart, and employees
- Manager of information
- Manager of time
- Manager of behavior
- Storyteller
- Note taker
- Numbers person (statistics)
- Listener (key item)
- Observer (key item)
- Quick study
- Trusted by ratifiers
- Trusted by own committee
- Trusted by key counterparts
- Trusted by others who affect decisions
- Good draftsperson
- Manager of caucuses

Tom Colosi's 10 Commandments of Negotiation

1. Appreciate that the essence of negotiation is an opportunity to exchange promises and commitments in an effort to resolve problems and reach agreement. *Appreciate also that this promise exchange is conducted in an environment devoid of rules of engagement.*

2. *Use active listening skills, such as open-ended questions, and paraphrasing, to arrive at the underlying "real" issues and interests only after negotiating the rules of engagement or "ground rules."*

3. *Appreciate the complexity of the negotiation process, which includes negotiations* on several levels: 1) across the table; 2) internal to the negotiating team; 3) internal to the organization; and 4) between the negotiators and their ratifiers.

4. *Understand that your job is to create doubts in your counterparts* about the viability of their interests and objectives. Understand that you can only effectively create doubts when you have developed trust and credibility and are believable.

5. *Always avoid surprises unless you can predict with deadly accuracy the reaction of the other side to your behavior,* resulting implications of the surprise, and that the surprise will actually advance your interests.

6. *Appreciate that an ethic in negotiation is to tell the truth, nothing but the truth, but not necessarily the whole truth since the management of information is essential to negotiation strategy.* This is also helpful because you should avoid negotiating serious/sensitive issues in the initially low-trust environment of the negotiation table. Work to create a healthy off-the-record process built on trust and credibility in which you can work on sensitive, high-concern issues.

7. Appreciate that the skilled negotiator is less like a gladiator and more like a mediator. Never quarrel or attempt to alienate your counterparts at the table. *Your counterparts are not your opponents*

but rather potential advocates for your interests as they negotiate with their ratifier.

8. *A key part of your role is to build trust while managing the expectations of the other parties.* Since most negotiators do not have the authority to ratify their own deals, during the course of the negotiation the negotiator should never make a promise to act, but only a promise to make a recommendation to his/her ratifier.

9. *Arrive at agreements by seeking to meet the underlying interests of all the parties and their constituents.* Appreciate that a "win/win" outcome is an ideal but rarely possible outcome. An "I can live with it—I can live with it" outcome is much more realistic.

10. *Appreciate that the implementation of the negotiated agreement is paramount.* Agreements should be fair, durable, and reality-checked for feasibility before being ratified so as not to damage the trust built among the parties.

Selected Bibliography

Acuff, Frank L. *How to Negotiate Anything with Anyone Anywhere Around the World*. New York: AMACOM, 1997.

Bandler, Richard, et. al. *Reframing: Neuro-Linguistic Programming and the Transformation of Meaning*. Moab, UT: Real People Press, 1988.

Bartos, O. *Process and Outcome of Negotiations*. New York: Columbia University Press, 1974.

Bazerman, Max H. and Roy J. Lewicki, eds. *Negotiating in Organizations*. Beverly Hills: Sage Publications, 1983.

Bazerman, Max H. and Margaret Ann Neale. *Negotiating Rationally*. New York: Free Press/Maxwell Macmillan, 1992.

Beckmann, Neal W. *Negotiations: Principles and Techniques*. Lexington, MA: D.C. Heath & Co., 1977.

Beer, Jennifer, et. al. *Mediator's Handbook*. Kingston, RI: New Society Publishers, Ltd., 1997.

Brams, Steven J. and Alan D. Taylor. *Win-Win Solution: Guaranteeing Fair Shares to Everybody*. New York: W.W. Norton, 1999.

Bramson, Robert, PhD and Allen F. Harrison, DPA. *The Styles of Thinking*. New York: Berkley Books, 1982.

Brock, Jonathan. *Bargaining Beyond Impasse: Joint Resolution of Public Sector Labor Disputes*. Dover, MA: Auburn House Publishing Co., 1986.

Calero, Henry H. *Winning the Negotiation*. New York: Hawthorn Books, 1990.

Carpenter, Susan S. and W.D.J. Kennedy. *Managing Public Disputes*. San Francisco/London: Jossey-Bass Publishers, 1988.

Coffin, Royce A. *The Negotiator: A Manual for Winners*. New York: Amacom, 1973.

Cohen, Herb. *You Can Negotiate Anything*. Secaucus, NJ: Lyle Stuart, 1980.

Cohen, Raymond. *Negotiating Across Cultures*. Washington, DC: U.S. Institute of Peace Press, 1991.

Cohen, Richard, ed. *Mediation...an Alternative that Works* (2nd ed.). Salem, MA: District Court Dept., Trial Court of Massachusetts, 1984.

Colosi, Thomas R. and Jeffrey G. Miller. *Fundamentals of Negotiation: A Guide for Environmental Professionals*. Washington, DC: Environmental Law Institute, 1989.

_____. "Negotiation in the Public and Private Sectors," *American Behavioral Scientist*, vol. 27, no. 2, (November -December 1983), pp. 229-253.

_____ and Arthur E. Berkeley. *Collective Bargaining: How it Works and Why* (2nd ed.). New York: American Arbitration Association, 1986.

_____ and Gregory A. Joseph. *Negotiating the Rules for Debate*. New York: American Arbitration Association, 1984.

Cooley, John W. "Arbitration vs. Mediation—It's Time to Settle the Differences," *Chicago Bar Record*, vol. 66, no. 4 (January-February 1985), pp. 204-221.

Coulson, Robert. *Business Arbitration: What You Need to Know* (3rd ed.). New York: American Arbitration Association, 1987.

_____. *How to Stay Out of Court* (2nd ed.). New York: American Arbitration Association, 1984.

_____. *Labor Arbitration: What You Need to Know* (3rd ed.). New York: American Arbitration Association, 1986.

_____. *Professional Mediation of Civil Disputes*. New York: American Arbitration Association, 1984.

Craver, Charles B. *Effective Legal Negotiation and Settlement*. Virginia: The Michie Company, 1986.

Curry, Jeffrey E. *A Short Course in International Business Negotiating: Planning and Conducting International Commercial Negotiations*. San Rafael, CA: World Trade Press, 1998.

Davis, Tom H. "Settlement Negotiations," *Trial* (July 1983), pp. 82-85, 120.

Druckman, Daniel and R. Mahoney. "Processes and Consequences of International Negotiations," *Journal of Social Issues*, vol. 33, no. 1 (1977), pp. 60-67.

Dunlop, John T. *Dispute Resolution: Negotiation and Consensus Building.* Dover, MA: Auburn House Publishing, 1984.

Edwards, Harry T. *The Lawyer as Negotiator: Problems, Readings and Materials.* St. Paul, MN: West Publishing, 1976.

Elkouri, Frank and Edna Asper Elkouri. *How Arbitration Works.* Washington, DC: The Bureau of National Affairs, Inc., 1985.

Elkouri, Frank, et al. *How Arbitration Works: Elkouri and Elkouri.* Washington, DC: BNA Books, 1997.

Fisher, Glen. *The Cross-Cultural Dimension in International Negotiation.* Prepared for School of Area Studies, Foreign Service Institute, U. S. Department of State, 1979.

Fisher, Roger and Scott Brown. *Getting Together: Building Relationships As We Negotiate.* New York: Viking Penguin, 1989.

Fisher, Roger, Elizabeth Kopelman, and Andrea Kupfer Schneider. *Beyond Machiavelli: Tools for Coping with Conflict.* Cambridge, MA: Harvard University Press, 1994.

Fisher, Roger and William Ury. *Getting to Yes* (2nd ed.). Boston: Houghton-Mifflin Co., 1991.

Folberg, Jay and Alison Taylor. *Mediation: A Comprehensive Guide to Resolving Conflicts Without Litigation.* San Francisco/London: Jossey-Bass Publishers, 1988.

Ghauri, Pervez N. and Jean-Claude Usunier. *International Business Negotiations.* New York: Pergamon, 1996.

Goldberg, Stephen B., Eric D. Green and Frank E. A. Sander. *Dispute Resolution.* Boston: Little, Brown and Company, 1985.

Gotbaum, Victor. *Negotiating in the Real World: Getting the Deal You Want.* New York: Simon & Schuster, 1999.

Guernsey, Thomas F. *A Practical Guide to Negotiation*. South Bend, IN: National Institute for Trial Advocacy, Notre Dame Law School, 1996.

Guetzkow, Harold and Jack Sawyer. "Bargaining and Negotiations in International Relations," *International Behavior: A Social-Psychological Analysis*, edited by Herbert C. Kelman. New York: Rinehart and Winston, 1966, pp. 466-520.

Gulliver, P.H. *Disputes and Negotiations: A Cross-Cultural Perspective*. New York: Academic Press, 1979.

Hall, Edward T. *The Hidden Dimension*. New York: Doubleday, 1966.

_____. *The Silent Language*. New York: Doubleday, 1959.

Hall, Joan. "Negotiation: Dispute Resolution as an Effective Alternative to Trial," *American Journal of Trial Advocacy*, vol. 6, no. 3 (Spring 1983), pp. 481-484.

Hall, Lavinia. *Negotiation Strategies for Mutual Gain: The Basic Seminar of the Harvard Program on Negotiation*. Newbury Park: Sage, 1993.

Hamner, Clay W. "Effects of Bargaining Strategy and Pressure to Reach an Agreement in a Stalemated Negotiation," *Journal of Personality and Social Psychology*, vol. 30 (October 1974), pp. 58-467.

Hawver, Dennis A. "Plan Before Negotiating...and Increase Your Power of Persuasion," *Management Review*, vol. 73, no. 2 (February 1984), pp. 46-48.

Heller, Deborah and David E. Berlew. "Negotiation Skills—Tools for Professional & Personal Success," *Legal Administrator*, vol. 3, no. 3 (Spring 1984), pp. 18-21.

Hendon, Donald W., Rebecca Angeles Hendon, and Paul A. Herbig. *Cross-Cultural Business Negotiations*. Westport, CT: Quorum, 1996.

Hodgson, James D., Yoshihiro Sano, and John L. Graham. *Doing Business with the New Japan*. Lanham, MD: Rowman & Littlefield Publishers, 2000.

Ikle, Fred C. *How Nations Negotiate*. New York: Harper and Row, 1964.

Illich, J. *The Art and Skill of Successful Negotiation*. Englewood Cliffs, NJ: Prentice-Hall, 1973.

Jandt, Fred E. *Win/Win Negotiating: Turning Conflict into Agreement.* New York: John Wiley & Sons, Inc., 1985.

Jonsson. *Soviet Bargaining Behavior: The Nuclear Test Ban Case.* Columbia, 1979.

Kagel, Sam. *Anatomy of a Labor Arbitration* (2nd ed.). Washington, DC: Bureau of National Affairs, 1986.

Kanowitz, Leo. *Alternative Dispute Resolution.* St. Paul, MN: West Publishing Company, 1986.

Karass, Chester L. *Give and Take.* New York: Thomas Y. Crowell Co., 1974.

_____. *The Negotiation Game.* New York: World Publishing, 1973.

Kaufman, Johan. *Conference Diplomacy.* Dobbs Ferry, NY: Oceana Publications, Inc., 1970.

Kochan, Thomas A., Mordehai Mironi, Ronald G. Ehrenberg, Jean Baderschneider and Todd Jick. *Dispute Resolution Under Fact-finding and Arbitration.* New York: American Arbitration Association, 1979.

Kolb, Deborah and Judith Williams. *The Shadow Negotiation: How Women Can Master the Hidden Agendas that Determine Bargaining Success.* New York: Simon & Schuster, 2000.

Kremenyuk, Victor A., ed. *International Negotiation: Analysis, Approaches, Issues.* San Francisco/Oxford: Jossey-Bass Publishers, 1991.

Kritek, Phyllis Beck. *Negotiating at an Uneven Table: A Practical Approach to Working with Difference and Diversity.* San Francisco: Jossey-Bass Inc., 1996.

Kublin, Michael. *International Negotiating: A Primer for American Business Professionals.* New York: International Business Press, 1995.

Kuechle, David. "The Art of Negotiation—An Essential Management Skill," *Business Quarterly* (October 1982, Special Supplement), pp. 9-22.

Lax, David A. and James K. Sebenius. *The Manager as Negotiator.* New York: The Free Press, division of MacMillan, Inc., 1986.

Lewicki, Roy J. *Negotiation: Readings, Exercises, and Cases.* Homewood, IL: Richard D. Irwin, 1985.

_____ et al. *Essentials of Negotiation.* New York: McGraw-Hill, 2000.

_____, Alexander Hiam, and Karen Olander. *Think Before You Speak: The Complete Guide to Strategic Negotiation.* New York: J. Wiley, 1996.

_____ and Joseph A. Litterer. *Negotiation.* Homewood, IL: Richard D. Irwin, 1985.

_____, David M. Saunders, and John W. Minton. *Negotiation.* Boston: Irwin/McGraw-Hill, 1999.

Loevi, Francis J. Jr., and Roger P. Kaplan. *Arbitration and the Federal Sector Advocate* (2nd ed.). New York: American Arbitration Association, 1982.

Main, Jeremy. "How to Be a Better Negotiator," *Fortune* (Sept. 19, 1983), pp. 141-142, 144, 146.

Marks, Jonathan B., Earl Johnson Jr. and Peter L. Szanton. *Dispute Resolution in America: Process in Evolution.* Washington, DC: The National Institute for Dispute Resolution, 1984.

Maurer, Robert. "How Successful People Succeed," and "The Pros and Cons of Conflict," from Maurer's "The Science of Excellence" lecture series. Information about Maurer's lectures and seminars is available through his Web site (www.robertmaurer.com).

McDonald, John W. *How to Be a Delegate.* Washington, DC: Foreign Service Institute of the U.S. Department of State, 1984.

_____ and Diane B. Bendahmane. *Conflict Resolution: Track Two Diplomacy.* Washington, DC: Foreign Service Institute of the U.S. Department of State, 1987.

_____ and Diane B. Bendahmane. *International Negotiation* (Art and Science). Washington, DC: Foreign Service Institute of the U.S. Department of State, 1984.

_____ and Diane B. Bendahmane. *Perspectives on Negotiation.* Washington, DC: Foreign Service Institute of the U.S. Department of State, 1984.

Mitchell, C.R. *Peacemaking and the Consultant's Role.* New York: Nichols Publishing Co., 1981.

Mnookin, Robert H., Lawrence Susskind, and Pacey C. Foster. *Negotiating on Behalf of Others: Advice to Lawyers, Business Executives, Sports Agents, Diplomats, Politicians, and Everybody Else.* Thousand Oaks, CA: Sage Publications, 1999.

Moberly, Ronald L. "Preparation for Negotiations," *Personnel Journal* (January 1978), pp. 36-39, 44.

Moore, Christopher W. *The Mediation Process: Practical Strategies for Resolving Conflict.* San Francisco/ London: Jossey-Bass Publishers, 1986.

Morse, Bruce. *How to Negotiate the Labor Agreement.* California: Trends Publishing Co., 1988.

Neal, Richard G. *Negotiations Strategies: A Reference Manual for Public Sector Labor Negotiations.* Richard Neal Associates, 1981.

Nierenberg, Gerard I. *Fundamentals of Negotiating.* New York: Hawthorn Books, Inc., 1973.

_____. *The Art of Negotiating.* New York: Simon & Schuster, 1968.

Nolan, Dennis R. *Labor Arbitration Law and Practice in a Nutshell.* St. Paul, MN: West Publishing, 1979.

_____. *Meta Talk.* New York: Simon and Schuster, 1973.

_____. *The Art of Negotiating: Psychological Strategies for Gaining Advantageous Bargains.* New York: Hawthorn Books, 1968.

Peterson, Craig A. and Claire McCarthy. *Arbitration Strategy and Technique.* Charlottesville, VA: The Michie Company, 1984 (includes 1987 supplement).

Phillips, Barbara Ashley and Anthony C. Piazza. "Using Mediation to Resolve Disputes," *California Lawyer*, vol. 3, no. 10 (October 1983), pp. 11-13.

Pruitt, Dean G. *Negotiatiwon Behavior.* New York: Academic Press, 1981.

Raiffa, Howard. *Lectures on Negotiation Analysis.* Cambridge, MA: PON Books, 1997.

_____. *The Art and Science of Negotiation.* Cambridge, MA: Harvard University Press, 1981.

Reychler, Luc. *Patterns of Diplomatic Thinking: A Cross-National Study of Structural and Social-Psychological Determinants*. New York: Praeger, 1979.

Riskin, Leonard L. and J. Westbrook, *Dispute Resolution and Lawyers*. St. Paul, MN. West Publishing, 1987.

Rogers, Nancy H. and Craig A. McEwen. *Mediation: Law, Policy, Practice*. Deerfield, IL: Clark Boardman Callaghan, 1989.

Sandole, Dennis J.D. and Ingrid Sandole-Staroste, eds. *Conflict Management and Problem Solving: Interpersonal to International Application*. London: Frances Pinter Publishers, 1987.

Schelling, Thomas C. *Strategy of Conflict*. Cambridge, MA: Harvard University Press, 1960.

Seltz, D. and A. Modica. *Negotiate Your Way to Success*. New York: Berkeley Publishing Corp., 1981.

Shell, G. Richard. *Bargaining for Advantage: Negotiation Strategies for Reasonable People*. New York: Viking Press, 1999.

Sinicropi, Anthony and Thomas P. Gilroy. *Collective Negotiations and Public Administration*. Iowa City, IA: Iowa City University, 1970.

Sperber, Philip. *Fail-Safe Business Negotiating*. Englewood Cliffs, NJ: Prentice-Hall, 1983.

Strauss, Anslem. *Negotiations: Varieties, Contexts, Processes, and Social Order*. San Francisco: Jossey-Bass, 1978.

Susskind, Lawrence and Jeffrey Cruikshank. *Breaking the Impasse: Consensual Approaches to Resolving Public Disputes*. New York: Basic Books, Inc., 1987.

Swartz, Herbert. "Structured Negotiations Save Time, Money and Blood Pressure," *Electronic Business*, vol. 10, no. 9 (June 1984), pp. 72, 74.

Thompson, Leigh L. *The Mind and Heart of the Negotiator*. Upper Saddle River, NJ: Prentice Hall, 1998.

Ury, William L., Jeanne M. Brett and Stephen B. Goldberg. *Getting Disputes Resolved*. San Francisco/London: Jossey-Bass Publishers, 1988.

_____. *Getting Past No: How to Deal with Difficult People*. New York: Bantam Books, 1991.

Vope, Maria R. and Thomas F. Christian, eds. *Problem Solving Through Mediation.* Washington, DC: Special Committee on Dispute Resolution, American Bar Association, 1983.

_____ and Joyce E. Kowaleski, eds. *Mediation in the Justice System.* Washington, DC: Special Committee on Dispute Resolution of the Public Services Division, American Bar Association, 1983.

Walton, Richard E. and Robert E. McKersie. *A Behavorial Theory of Labor Negotiations: An Analysis of a Social Interaction System.* New York: McGraw-Hill Book, Co., 1965.

Wenke, Robert A. *The Art of Negotiation for Lawyers.* Long Beach, CA: Richter Publications, 1985.

Westin, Alan F. and Alfred G. Feliu. *Resolving Employment Disputes Without Litigation.* Washington, DC: The Bureau of National Affairs, Inc., 1988.

Williams, Gerald R. *Legal Negotiation and Settlement.* St. Paul, MN: West Publishing, 1983.

Zack, Arnold M. *Arbitration in Practice.* New York: Cornell University, 1984.

_____, ed. *The Negotiation Process: Theories and Applications.* Beverly Hills, CA: Sage Publications, Inc., 1978.

_____ and M. Berman. "How Diplomats Negotiate," Mimeographed, AED, 1976.

Zartman, I. William. "Processes of International Negotiation Project and International Institute for Applied Systems Analysis," *International Multilateral Negotiation: Approaches to the Management of Complexity.* San Francisco: Jossey-Bass, 1994.

_____, ed. *The 50% Solution: How to Bargain Successfully with Hijackers, Strikers, Bosses, Oil Magnates, Arabs, Russians, and Other Worthy Opponents in this Modern World.* Garden City, NY: Doubleday Anchor Press, 1976.

_____ and Maureen R. Berman. *The Practical Negotiator.* New Haven, CT: Yale University Press, 1982.

Zeckhauser, Richard, Ralph L. Keeney, and James K. Sebenius. *Wise Choices: Decisions, Games, and Negotiations.* Boston: Harvard Business School Press, 1996.